Getting Started RPA Using Automation Anywhere

Automate Your Day-to-Day Business
Processes Using Automation Anywhere

Vaibhav Srivastava

www.bpbonline.com

FIRST EDITION 2021

Copyright © BPB Publications, India

ISBN: 978-93-89898-286

Distributors:

BPB PUBLICATIONS
20, Ansari Road, Darya Ganj
New Delhi-110002
Ph: 23254990/23254991

DECCAN AGENCIES
4-3-329, Bank Street,
Hyderabad-500195
Ph: 24756967/24756400

MICRO MEDIA
Shop No. 5, Mahendra Chambers,
150 DN Rd. Next to Capital Cinema,
V.T. (C.S.T.) Station, MUMBAI-400 001
Ph: 22078296/22078297

BPB BOOK CENTRE
376 Old Lajpat Rai Market,
Delhi-110006
Ph: 23861747

To View Complete
BPB Publications Catalogue
Scan the QR Code:

Published by Manish Jain for BPB Publications, 20 Ansari Road, Darya Ganj, New Delhi-110002 and Printed by him at Repro India Ltd, Mumbai

Dedicated to

Sushil, Amita, Shubhangi, Rankita, and Shooleen Srivastava
My family, which has been always my support system.

About the Author

Vaibhav is a Software Delivery Manager, with 11 years of experience in which he has implemented multiple assignments with varying roles like architect, business analyst, solution consultant, and instructor for various technologies like RPA, data science, machine learning, and .NET.

Some of the organizations that Vaibhav has been associated with are ContactPoint360, IBM, HPE, KPMG, Novartis, Unisys, TCL, HCL Technologies, Ryan India, and NSEIT to name a few.

In 2017, Vaibhav moved into RPA and started his journey with Automation Anywhere. The journey has been a cherished one and has taken him on multiple unexplored areas. After Automation Anywhere, Vaibhav also developed expertise in UiPath, another market-leading RPA tool, and later upgraded tech stack with gaining knowledge about machine learning, data science, and artificial intelligence.

Outside work, Vaibhav volunteers his spare time in helping, coaching, and mentoring young people in taking up careers in technology.

Acknowledgement

There are a few people I want to thank for the continued and ongoing support they have given me during the writing of this book. First and foremost, I would like to thank my family and daughter, Shooleen, for putting up with me while I was spending many weekends and evenings on writing—I could have never completed this book without their support.

Finally, I would like to thank BPB Publications for giving me this opportunity to write my first book for them.

Preface

Robotic process automation is a software development environment using which one can create robots that mimic human actions on different business applications (CRMs, ERPs, help desk, and claim applications).

According to the Institute of Robotic Process Automation and Artificial Intelligence (IRPA AI), RPA is the application of technology that allows employees in a company to configure a computer software or a "robot" to capture and interpret the existing applications for processing a transaction, manipulating data, triggering responses, and communicating with other digital systems.

Robotics refers to the software robots, and robotics ascribes to the physical or humanoid robots.

RPA is the base level or stepping stone into the business process automation. The business processes that are automated using RPA are rule-based, repetitive, and mundane and work on the structured data. The process cannot have a touchpoint that requires the use of human intelligence or requires the bot to make judgement calls.

Automation using cognitive capabilities is the second level of business process automation. Cognitive Automation is like teaching a child. While creating cognitive automation, we train the bot to identify and learn different variations in the process. The processes that should be automated where there are variations in business rules and the variations are in the limit that those can be trained to a robot. Cognitive Automation is created by using machine learning.

Automation using artificial intelligence is the third level of automation. Automation created using AI is very similar to a human doing a process that involves a high level of human intelligence and judgement calls. The processes primed for AI Automation can be preparing legal arguments for a court case studying previous judgements or providing the most suitable medicine based on the symptoms to doctors.

The primary goal of this book is to provide the information and skills that are necessary to develop and deploy bots created in Automation Anywhere environment. This book contains real-life case studies and their practical implementation that will show you how to develop, deploy, and schedule bots as well as create secure the credential variables and workflow. Over the 14 chapters in this book, you will learn the following:

Chapter 1 discusses business process automation, its advantages, and the stages of business process automation, namely, RPA, cognitive automation, and augmented artificial intelligence.

Chapter 2 discusses robotic process automation, how it is different from traditional automation, a checklist for selecting RPA tool, and RPA tools in market and their use cases.

Chapter 3 discusses the architecture of Automation Anywhere Enterprise application and its components, namely, Bot Creator, Web Control Room and Bot Runner.

Chapter 4 is about the client application, which is the interface for Bot Creator and Bot Runner and the functionality and options available to each of the role.

Chapter 5 is a key chapter that discusses, in-depth, about variables and mainly user variables and its types which are value, list, array, random, and dictionary. It also provides step-by-step practical exercises that help you understand how and when to use each of the variable types.

Chapter 6 is also a key chapter that provides a step-by-step practical implementation of industry use cases. The use cases implemented are excel data processing, web data extractor, share price infuser, database data extractor, and invoice processing.

Chapter 7 discusses the commands provided in the command library. Some of the important commands discussed are FTP, Keystrokes, String Operation, XML, and more.

Chapter 8 describes how to create and use reusable components and Metabot and its advantages. It also describes how to use Citrix AISense technology to capture the objects in citrix, virtual machine, and remote environment.

Chapter 9 discusses the three recorders provided in Automation Anywhere, namely, screen, web, and smart recorder and how to use them.

Chapter 10 describes how to create and consume the credential variables that are used to store sensitive data in a secured locker.

Chapter 11 describes a step-by-step development and implementation of IQ bots that are used to add cognitive capabilities to the bots.

Chapter 12 discusses workflows that are graphical environments provided by Automation Anywhere to define the process flow.

Chapter 13 discusses logging and monitoring mechanism provided as system and audit logs.

Chapter 14 discusses the steps to upload/download or transfer the bots and the steps to schedule bots from the Web Control Room to be executed on the Bot Runner.

Downloading the coloured images:

Please follow the link to download the
Coloured Images of the book:

https://rebrand.ly/s795cp5

Errata

We take immense pride in our work at BPB Publications and follow best practices to ensure the accuracy of our content to provide with an indulging reading experience to our subscribers. Our readers are our mirrors, and we use their inputs to reflect and improve upon human errors, if any, that may have occurred during the publishing processes involved. To let us maintain the quality and help us reach out to any readers who might be having difficulties due to any unforeseen errors, please write to us at :

errata@bpbonline.com

Your support, suggestions and feedbacks are highly appreciated by the BPB Publications' Family.

Did you know that BPB offers eBook versions of every book published, with PDF and ePub files available? You can upgrade to the eBook version at www.bpbonline.com and as a print book customer, you are entitled to a discount on the eBook copy. Get in touch with us at :

business@bpbonline.com for more details.

At **www.bpbonline.com**, you can also read a collection of free technical articles, sign up for a range of free newsletters, and receive exclusive discounts and offers on BPB books and eBooks.

BPB is searching for authors like you

If you're interested in becoming an author for BPB, please visit **www.bpbonline.com** and apply today. We have worked with thousands of developers and tech professionals, just like you, to help them share their insight with the global tech community. You can make a general application, apply for a specific hot topic that we are recruiting an author for, or submit your own idea.

The code bundle for the book is also hosted on GitHub at **https://github.com/bpbpublications/Getting-Started-with-RPA-Using-Automation-Anywhere**. In case there's an update to the code, it will be updated on the existing GitHub repository.

We also have other code bundles from our rich catalog of books and videos available at **https://github.com/bpbpublications**. Check them out!

PIRACY

If you come across any illegal copies of our works in any form on the internet, we would be grateful if you would provide us with the location address or website name. Please contact us at **business@bpbonline.com** with a link to the material.

If you are interested in becoming an author

If there is a topic that you have expertise in, and you are interested in either writing or contributing to a book, please visit **www.bpbonline.com**.

REVIEWS

Please leave a review. Once you have read and used this book, why not leave a review on the site that you purchased it from? Potential readers can then see and use your unbiased opinion to make purchase decisions, we at BPB can understand what you think about our products, and our authors can see your feedback on their book. Thank you!

For more information about BPB, please visit **www.bpbonline.com**.

Table of Contents

CHAPTER 1
Introduction to Business Process Automation

Introduction

In this chapter, we will discuss why to automate the business processes. We'll also discuss the stages of automation that are robotic process automation, cognitive automation, and artificial intelligence augmentation.

Structure

In this chapter, we will discuss the following topics:

- Business process automation
- Stages of business process automation, namely,
  - o   Robotic process automation
  - o   Cognitive automation
  - o   Augmented artificial intelligence

Objectives

After completing this chapter, you should be able to:

- Understand business process automation
- Understand the advantages of business process automation
- Understand the stages of business process automation

Business process automation

Every business built and which operates at a scale works on well-defined processes. These processes allow the organization to streamline each and every aspect of the business.

Some examples of the process in an organization are:

- **Employee onboarding**: A new employee joins the company; their details are saved in the employee data repository, login and access are created for them; and their credentials are shared with them.

- **Invoice processing**: Vendors send the invoice through the email. Each invoice is downloaded, and then the invoice data is extracted one by one from each invoice. The extracted data is then saved and shared via email to the concerned person/department.

- **Data processing**: The records 1are saved in an excel sheet. The FTE opens the excel sheet, reads the record row by row, and feeds the data into a web or desktop application which in turn saves the data into a data store like a database.

Most of these processes are repetitive in nature, are mundane, and do not require any judgment calls. The human resource or employee involved in doing these processes is doing the same thing again and again, for hours, day in and day out for years without utilizing much of the best processing power available in the world, their brain.

This leads to an employee feeling that he/she is not being utilized to their full potential. The employee productivity degrades over time; and the attitude towards the organization doesn't remain healthy. This is one of the prime reasons for a very large part of the workforce being frustrated, impacting the health and wealth of the employee, seniors, and the organization overall.

When an organization looks at the productivity of the employees, the picture isn't rosy as well. The employees have their own set of demands. The organization spends a lot of money creating the peripheral infrastructure around the employee like the cafeteria, recreation room, and so on. Then, the employees take a lunch break, coffee/ tea breaks, and so on.

The employees being human would have some error in their work. So, the work of one employee has to be rechecked and verified by another employee. The employees also require leaves and are available only for a limited time in the 24-hour day cycle.

The organizations know that a lot of a time for which employees are paid is wasted in non-productive works by employees. This further creates mistrust and deteriorates the working relationship between the organization and the employee. The issues mentioned are solved by **automating processes** or **business process automation**.

Business process automation is a technology to develop and deploy software robots that interact with applications imitating human actions. Business process automation can be categorized under three stages, which are explained in the following sections.

Robotic process automation

Robotic process automation (RPA) is the base level or stepping stone into business process automation. The business processes that are automated using RPA are rule-based, repetitive, and mundane in nature and work on structured data. The process cannot have touchpoints that require the use of human intelligence or require the bot to take the judgement calls.

Some examples of RPA are automating the tasks that are straight forward and do not have variations in the business rules. The processes primed for robotic process automation have business rules clearly defined and structured data for input and the expected automated response mentioned.

Cognitive automation

Automation using cognitive capabilities is the second level of business process automation. Cognitive Automation is like teaching a child. While creating cognitive automation, we train the bot to identify and learn different variations in the process.

Let us say there is a business process in which the data has to be extracted from multiple invoices sent by different vendors. As of now, we will concentrate only on one field, the invoice number. Some vendor writes *Invoice Number* as *Invoice #* in their invoices. Some of them write Invoice number as *Invoice No,* and some write *Invoice number* as *Invoice Number*. Some write the Invoice number at the top of the invoice, some at the bottom. Some give the Invoice number at the left section of the invoice, some to the right. Now, there are multiple variations for the same field to be captured with no fixed structure.

In the previously discussed scenario, we can use cognitive automation. We can train the robot to learn and identify that *Invoice Number, Invoice No,* and *Invoice #* are the same field with a different variation. We can train the robot that this field has to be captured in whichever section of the invoice it exists.

The processes that should be automated where there are variations in business rules and the variations are in the limit that those can be trained to a robot. Cognitive automation is created by using machine learning, natural language processing, computer vision, and fuzzy logic.

Artificial intelligence augmentation

Automation using Artificial Intelligence is the third level of automation. Automation created using AI is similar to a human doing a process that involves a high level of human intelligence and judgment calls. The processes primed for AI automation can be preparing legal arguments for a court case studying the previous judgments or providing the most suitable medicine based on the symptoms to the doctors.

Some companies have already created their AI engines and are being used for automating the processes in their organizations and their organizations as well. IBM has created its AI engine which is named Watson. SAP has developed its own AI engine named Leonardo.

Business process automation market share

According to the HfS Research 2017 study, the combined expenditure by organizations on RPA, Intelligent (Cognitive) Automation, and AI was $5.8 billion in 2016. In 2021, the combined expenditure on RPA, Intelligent (Cognitive) Automation, and AI will be $15.4 billion.

Year	RPA	Intelligent Process Automation	AI Business Operations
2016	$ 0.3 bn	$ 4.8 bn	$ 0.7 bn
2017	$ 0.4 bn	$ 6.2 bn	$ 1.1 bn
2018	$ 0.6 bn	$ 7.5 bn	$ 1.6 bn
2019	$ 0.8 bn	$ 8.9 bn	$ 2.0 bn
2020	$ 1 bn	$ 10.2 bn	$ 2.4 bn
2021	$ 1.2 bn	$ 11.5 bn	$ 2.7 bn

Table 1.1: HfS Research Automation & AI Growth

This level of expenditure will lead to the creation of a lot of jobs that will require a workforce with the requisite skills. So, the professionals who acquire or reskill themselves with the required skill set will be able to present themselves for the opportunities being created by the business process automation.

Conclusion

In this chapter, we discussed why the business process should be automated. We discussed the issues that are solved by automating business processes. The three stages of automation which are robotic process automation, cognitive automation, and artificial intelligence augmentation were also discussed. We also discussed the business process automation market share projected by the HfS research study.

We also learned about business process automation and the advantages of automating business processes.

In the next chapter, we will discuss robotic process automation, the factors to keep in mind while selecting an RPA tool for the organization, and the RPA tools available in the market.

Multiple choice questions

1. **Which stage of business process automation can be mimicked like teaching a child?**

    a. Robotic process automation

    b. Cognitive automation

    c. Artificial intelligence augmentation

    d. None of the above

2. **Which stage of business process automation is primed for automating repetitive processes?**

    a. Robotic process automation

    b. Cognitive automation

    c. Artificial intelligence augmentation

    d. None of the above

3. **Which is the name of the AI engine developed by IBM?**

    a. Leonardo

    b. SageMaker

    c. Watson

    d. None of the above

Answer

1. *b*

2. *a*

3. *c*

CHAPTER 2

Introduction to Robotic Process Automation

Introduction

In this chapter, we will discuss **robotic process automation (RPA)** and the difference between the traditional automation and robotic process automation. We will discuss the checklist for selecting the RPA tool and the RPA tools available in the market. We will also discuss the industry use cases primed for RPA.

Structure

In this chapter, we will discuss the following topics:

- Robotic process automation
- Difference between traditional automation and RPA
- RPA tool selection checklist
- RPA tools in the market
- Industry use cases

Objectives

After completing this chapter, you should be able to:

- Understand the robotic process automation

- Understand how traditional automation and RPA are different
- Understand processes that can be automated using RPA in different industries

Robotic process automation

When we talk about RPA, it consists of the following three terms:

- Robotic
- Process
- Automation

A process is a step of steps to complete a task to accomplish a defined outcome. Let us assume that the process to move from Point A to Point B. At the start, we used to do this process manually, by using our legs and walking or running. The automation of this process was done a long time back with the invention of the wheel. First came the bullock carts, and then came the bicycles, then bikes, cars, and airplanes. So, where does Robotic comes into picture? The introduction of software robots in the form of driverless cars, driverless trains, or autopilot brings robotic into the picture. I am not saying that driverless cars or autopilot are examples of RPA. Those are examples of an advanced level of Automation. I am saying these are examples of bring robotic (software robots) into the traditional automation.

RPA is a software development environment using which one can create robots that mimic human actions on different business applications (CRMs, ERPs, help desk, and claim applications).

According to *Institute of Robotic Process Automation & Artificial Intelligence (IRPAAI)*, RPA is the application of technology that allows the employees in a company to configure the computer software or a *robot* to capture and interpret the existing applications for processing a transaction, manipulating data, triggering responses, and communicating with other digital systems. When we talk about Robotic, there are two terms here: Robotic and Robotics.

Robotic refers to the software robots, and Robotics ascribe to the physical or humanoid robots. So, the robots that paint the cars in workshops or humanoid robots in restaurants are examples of Robotics. RPA is a robotic process automation, and here, we will be referring to the software robots.

Difference between traditional automation and RPA

Let us assume there is a complex mathematical equation to be solved. First, we used to solve this equation manually. Then, we did automation and invented a calculator to solve a complex mathematical equation. So, this mathematical equation to be solved is written on a piece of paper or text file on the system. A human reads the equation and provides the input to the calculator, and the calculator uses this input provided by humans and gives the automated response as output. This is how traditional automation works. This is the Pre RPA scenario.

In the Post RPA scenario, the mathematical equation will be read from the text file and passed to the calculator as an input by a robot by replacing the human effort, and then the calculator will do the rest of the process as earlier and provide an automated response.

Let us assume another use case. There's an excel sheet with certain company names and associated company codes. These are the codes provided by the stock exchange for each company to check the share price of the company on the stock exchange. In the excel sheet, there are 1000 companies, whose share price has to be searched and captured daily from the stock exchange web application and saved into the excel sheet:

	A	B	C	D
1	**Company**	Code	Price	
2	Infosys	INFY		
3	Wipro	WIPRO		
4	L & T Technology Services Limited	LTTS		
5				
6				
7				
8				
9				

Figure 2.1: Sample Excel Sheet with Company Name and Code

The share price data to be extracted from the web application is presented in the format provided as follows:

Infosys Limited
Series: EQ |

Symbol: INFY   ISIN: INE009A01021   Statu
Symbol P/E: 21.29   Sectoral Index P/E: 21.

733.10
▼ -2.90 -0.39%

Pr. Close
736.00

Figure 2.2: Company Share Price Data

An employee opens the excel sheet, reads the company name and code one by one, searches for it on the stock exchange web application, extracts the company share price, saves it into an excel sheet, and then sends the excel sheet as a mail attachment to the recipient(s). This is an example of traditional automation and the Pre RPA scenario.

We create a robot to replace the human effort in the previously mentioned process. So, the robot will read the company name and code one by one, search and extract the share price of each company from the stock exchange web application, and save the share price of each company in the excel sheet. Finally, the robot will send the excel sheet as a mail attachment to the recipient(s). This is the Post RPA scenario.

After the implementation of RPA, the human effort or human touchpoints in a business process are replaced by a software robot to leverage the existing business applications. RPA is used to *automate repetitive*, rule-based processes that have structured data. The advantages of using RPA are error-free automation, cost, and time-saving resulting in higher ROI and reduced human effort.

RPA growth trends

According to HfS Research 2018, the combined market of RPA Software and Services was $ 612 million in 2016, which has been taken as the base year. In 2017, the combined market gets a YoY growth rate of 63%, and the total volume is $ 1,114 million. By 2022, the combined market volume of the RPA Software and Services market is estimated to be $ 4,308 million by registering a YoY growth rate of 20%.

Year	RPA Software	RPA Services	RPA Software & Services
2016	$183m	$429m	$612m
2017	$315m	$799m	$1114m
2018	$461m	$1253m	$1714m
2019	$608m	$1736m	$2344m
2020	$755m	$2238m	$2993m
2021	$903m	$2750m	$3653m
2022	$1050m	$3258m	$4608m

Table 2.1: RPA Software and Services Market Growth Projection by Hfs in 2018

According to HfS Research 2018, North America leads the region-wise RPA market with the volume being $698 million and shares being 41%. Western Europe takes the second position with the volume being $480 million, and the market share is 28%. The third position is Asia with the volume being $386 million, and the market share being 22%. Asia is followed by Latin America, with the volume being $ 82 million and a market share of 5% and is just slightly ahead of Rest of the **Europe, Middle East, and Asia (EMEA),** which has a volume of 69 million and a market share of 4% as follows:

Region	Market volume	Market share (%)
North America	$698m	41
Latin America	$82m	5
Western Europe	$480m	28
Asia	$386m	22
Rest of EMEA	$69m	4

Table 2.2: Region-wise RPA Market Estimate by HfS in 2018

RPA tool selection checklist

When we have to select an RPA tool for the organization, there are several factors that have to be kept in mind. The factors are detailed as follows:

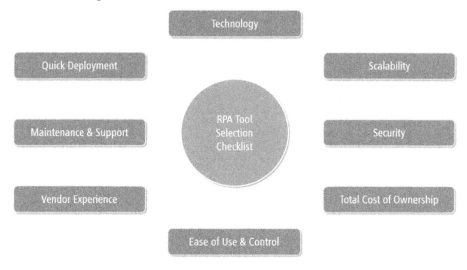

Figure 2.3: RPA Tool Selection Checklist

Let us discuss each of the RPA Tool Selection Checklist features as follows:

- **Technology:** The tool that is to be selected, whether it supports the technological architecture of the organization or the applications. If your organization has a lot of implementation of ERP like SAP or Oracle ERP, then the tool that you select has the capability to import/ export data in SAP or Oracle ERP. If your organization does a lot of PDF processing, does the tool have capabilities to process the PDF with a high precision? If the organization is a banking institution that provides multiple interactivity channels to clients like the mobile app, website, and so on where the data is exposed through Web APIs, then the tool that is selected needs to have the technological capability to interact the APIs.

- **Scalability:** The robots created by the tool that is selected for implementing RPA should be scalable at a larger level. Let us assume that the New York or the London or the Dubai or the Bangalore office of an organization has automated a process that is implemented at the global level across the organization. The tool that has to be selected should have the capability that the robot and the dependencies developed to automate the process can be scaled and shared with minimal efforts and changes with all the office locations of the organization. So, while selecting the RPA tool, we have to keep in mind that the tool should be capable of scaling up the RPA infrastructure and developed robots at a larger level.

- **Security:** In RPA tools, security is categorized as follows:
  - o **Role-based access:** While selecting the tool, we have to keep in mind whether the tool has the capability to provide specific privileges to certain groups or individuals or the tool has the capability for providing role-based access to the tool and its components. The tool should have the capability that the users can create their roles and a set of privileges other than the ones provided out of the box with the product installation.

  - o **Data security:** The tool once installed should have the organization data secure in its premises and should not send back any data to the **original product creator (OEM).** If the tool provides a cloud edition or a mobile app which have accounts for multiple organizations, then the multi-tenancy should be maintained or the data of each organization should be under separate accounts.

  - o **Secure credentials:** Let us assume there is a process to be automated in which login is required into multiple portals is required and then some action is performed on each of the portals. The details that are required to login to the portal are of the Project Manager. Will the Project Manager like to share his/her login details with a developer in the organization who can misuse his/her credentials? The answer to this question is No. So, the tool that is to be selected, in this scenario, should have the capability to securely save the login details of the Project Manager in encrypted form. The developer while creating the robot should be able to access the secure credentials for further automation, but the developer should not be able to see the actual values of the credentials.

- **Total cost of ownership:** The cost of ownership is one of the biggest factors while selecting an RPA tool for the organization. Most of the leading RPA tools are license based that have an annual renewal. Apart from that a lot of physical infrastructures and human resource cost is also involved. The ROI should be calculated beforehand and should justify the implementation and ownership cost of RPA.

- **Ease of use and control:** The next factor to keep in mind is that the learning curve and the cost for human resources for using the tool should not be steep. The creation of in-house capability to use and control the tool should be easy, and it should not be the case that for the handling of the majority of the operation in the tool, the OEM team is required.

- **Vendor experience:** The experience of the vendor or the partner organizations with the OEM of the tool should be an important criterion while selecting the tool. One should look into whether the vendor or partner feedback is asked and appreciated by the OEM. The just demands of the vendor or partner are obliged by the OEM or not.

- **Maintenance and support:** The time taken for the resolution of the problem, quality of the solution of the problem, the support provided in case of a version upgrade of the product in terms of migration or retraining of the resources, or providing hotfixes to issues in the product. These factors should also be kept in mind while selecting a tool for implementing RPA in the organization.

- **Quick deployment:** The time taken for the deployment of the tool and the components with all the integrations and the policy requirements and migration should also be considered while selecting the RPA tool for the organization.

RPA tools in the market

The following are some of the RPA tools available in the market:

- Automation Anywhere
- UiPath
- BluePrism
- Pegasystem
- NICE
- Kofax
- Softmotive
- Kryon
- AntWorks
- WorkFusion
- EdgeVerve
- AssistEdge

According to *Everest Group Research RPA Product PEAK Matrix Assessment 2019* report, Automation Anywhere and UiPath are star performers and top RPA tools in the market and are followed by BluePrism and NICE in the leader category.

There are a lot of RPA tools that are major contenders that can jump into the leader category as the OEMs of these RPA tools upgrade their capabilities. Some of the tools that are the base of the springboard to make the jump into the leader category are Kryon, Pegasystems, AntWorks, EdgeVerve, and another Monday among others and are backed by the giants of the industry as partners as follows:

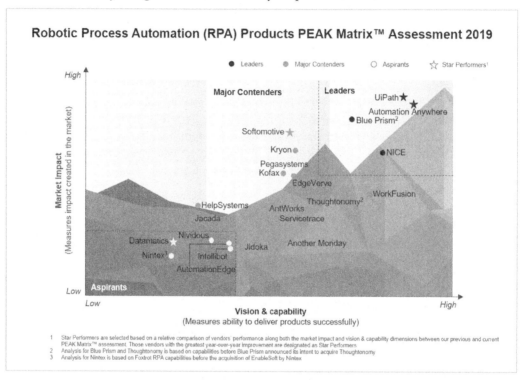

Figure 2.4: RPA Tool PEAK Assessment by Everest Group Research

Source: https://www2.everestgrp.com/reportaction/EGR-2019-38-R-3217/Marketing

RPA primed industry use cases

There are many processes under different domains and industries that can be automated using RPA. We will just discuss a few of them under some domains/industries as follows:

- **HR:** The employee onboarding, payroll management, bulk email notifications, and leave management can be some of the processes that can be automated in the HR domain.

- **BFSI:** Some of the processes that can be automated for **Banking, Financial Services & Insurance (BFSI)** industry could be insurance premium calculation, loan premium calculation, EMI payment reminder, customer onboarding, credit card issuance, uploading NAV data of the customers to the regulator portal on a daily, monthly, quarterly, and yearly basis, report generation, auditing, generating and emailing the customer bank statements, and so on to name a few.

- **Telecommunications:** Bill generation, customer helpline, and bill payment reminder are a few of the processes that can be automated.

- **Logging, monitoring, and troubleshooting:** Helpdesk operations, ticketing operations, auditing, data logging and monitoring of switches and routers, and so on can be some of the processes that can be automated using RPA. Ticketing tool like **Service Now (SNow)** has been automated end-to-end by a leading global organization.

- **Manufacturing:** Invoice processing, automating operations in ERP tools like SAP or Oracle ERP, extracting data from web portals, and creating reports based on the data and so on can be some of the processes for automation using RPA.

- **Healthcare:** Patient onboarding, Drug suggestion to the doctor based on patient symptoms, patient record storage and migration, drug testing assistance, and so on can be some of the processes for automation.

There are around 55-80% of the processes that can be automated using RPA based on the industry and domain. This provides the organization high ROI, error-free execution, lower **TAT (turnaround time),** and the workforce released can now be utilized into far more productive jobs.

Conclusion

In this chapter, we discussed Robotic Process Automation and what each term means and discussed the difference between robotic and robotics. We further discussed the difference between traditional automation and robotic process automation. We also discussed the factors to keep in mind while selecting an RPA tool and the RPA tools available in the market. We also discussed the industry use cases primed to be automated using the robotic process automation.

We also learned about the meaning of the terms in RPA, the difference between traditional and robotic process automation, RPA tool selection checklist factors, and the RPA tools available in the market.

In the next chapter, we will discuss the architecture of Automation Anywhere Enterprise software, Bot Creator, Web Control Room, and Bot Runner and how they are connected to each other.

Multiple choice questions

1. **Role-based access comes under which feature of RPA Selection checklist:**

   a. Technology

   b. Vendor experience

   c. Security

   d. None of the above

2. **Which stage of business process automation is primed for automating repetitive processes?**

   a. Robotic process automation

   b. Cognitive automation

   c. Artificial intelligence augmentation

   d. None of the above

3. **Which is the name of the AI engine developed by IBM?**

   a. Leonardo

   b. SageMaker

   c. Watson

   d. None of the above

Answer

1. *c*

2. *a*

3. *c*

CHAPTER 3

Automation Anywhere Enterprise Architecture

Introduction

In this chapter, we will discuss the three components of Automation Anywhere Enterprise software, namely, Bot Creator, which is the development component, Web Control Room, which is the governing or maintenance component, and Bot Runner, which is the execution component. We will also learn about the architecture of Automation Anywhere Enterprise software.

Structure

In this chapter, we will discuss the following topics:

- Automation Anywhere
- AAE Components
    - o Bot Creator
    - o Web Control Room
    - o Bot Runner
- AAE Architecture

Objectives

After completing this chapter, you should be able to:

- Understand the AAE Components, namely, Bot Creator, Web Control Room, and Bot Runner
- Understand the AAE Architecture and the communication methodology between bot creator, web control room, and bot runner

Automation Anywhere

Automation Anywhere is one of the popular RPA vendors offering powerful and user-friendly RPA capabilities to automate any complex tasks. It is one of the revolutionary technology that changes the way the enterprise operates. This tool combines conventional RPA with intellectual elements like cognitive capabilities and real-time business intelligence. The Automation Anywhere tool can automate end-to-end business operations for companies.

AAE components

There are three components of the Automation Anywhere Enterprise tool as follows:

- Bot Creator
- Web Control Room
- Bot Runner

AAE COMPONENTS

Figure 3.1: Automation Anywhere Enterprise Components

Bot Creator

The Bot Creator is the development component. All the robots that are created for automating the processes are created in the Bot Creator. The commands, variables, recorders, and so on are available under the Bot Creator.

Web Control Room

The Web Control Room is the governance or monitoring component. Reporting, auditing, scheduling, device pool management, queue management, user management, license management, role-based access, secure credentials, migration, versioning, and so on come under the Web Control Room.

Bot Runner

The Bot Runner is the execution component. The Bot runner is the standalone machine on which the real-time execution of the robot takes place. As a best practice, these should be a standalone machine on which no human interaction should be there. Let us say there is a robot executing on the bot runner automating a process, where the data is being copied and pasted using the keyboard shortcuts, namely, *Ctrl + C* and *Ctrl + V*. If any human is working on the same machine, then he/she can press any other key at the same time that can lead to runtime errors and ultimately failure of the robot. This is the reason for which the bot runner is kept as a standalone machine with no human interference in the real-time execution of robots.

Automation Anywhere Enterprise Architecture

The following is the architecture of Automation Anywhere:

AAE ARCHITECTURE

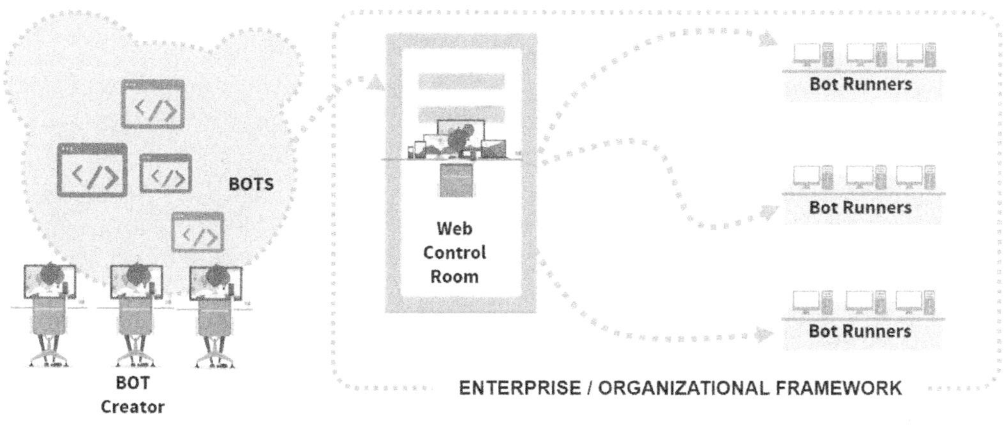

Figure 3.2: Automation Anywhere Enterprise Architecture

The Bot Creator and Bot Runner are connected with the Web Control Room with no direct communication between them. The robots (referred to as bots in the preceding figure) are created by the Bot Creator and then uploaded to the Web Control Room. In the Web Control Room, these robots are scheduled to be executed on the Bot Runners.

The Web Control Room and Bot Runner will always be under the organizational framework. The Bot Creator can be inside or outside the organization framework/ network. Many companies develop in-house robot development capability. In this scenario, the Bot Creator will also be inside the organizational framework. Some companies do not want to invest in the in-house robot development capability and outsource this work to other organizations. In this scenario, the Bot Creator will be outside the organizational framework. The robots will be developed by the development company and sent to the Web Control Room team in the organization through an email or any other mechanism, and then the Web Control Room team will upload the robots in the Web Control Room to be scheduled on the Bot Runners inside the organizational framework.

There could be scenarios for having multiple Bot Runners and Web Control Room. First, we will discuss the multiple Bot Runners scenario. Let us say on an average one robot takes 15 minutes to execute. Some robots might take 5 minutes to execute, and some might take 30 minutes, and the average time can be 15 minutes for the execution of the robots. So, on a single bot runner machine, 96 robots per day can be executed at the maximum (4 per hour * 24 hours). So, if we have more than 96 robots to be executed, then multiple bot runner machines would be required as on a single bot runner machine; only one robot can be executed at a given point of time. As the automation matures in any organization, the number of processes that have been automated for each domain/department or if the departments do not want to share their data with each other, then the departments can have single/multiple bot runner machines dedicated to them.

Let us assume there is an automated process that processes 10,000 rows of excel data. If this process is being executed on a single bot runner machine and processed on the 9,000th row , the bot runner machine goes down. Now, the process again has to start from Row 1. But if the process is being executed on multiple (assume three) bot runner machines (BR1, BR2, and BR3), then even if the BR1 machine goes down, the process will keep executing on BR2 and BR3. Also, this approach will bring down the total process execution time.

The scenario for having multiple Web Control Room could be load balancing, each department having its Web Control Room, or having separate testing and production Web Control Room.

Automation Anywhere Software Edition

There are two following versions of the Automation Anywhere software available, namely, Enterprise and Community edition:

- **Enterprise:** The Automation Anywhere Enterprise Edition is for big organizations, and it provides access to unlimited number of Bot Creators and Bot Runners (based on license) with full access to all features of the Web Control Room. The full access to the IQ bot development platform (license based) is provided with unlimited learning instances and processes. The license is an annual subscription.

- **Community:** The Automation Anywhere Community Edition is available for small businesses/developers/students. It provides a full access to the Bot Creator with all the features, access to limited features of Web Control room, and a Bot Runner Agent for the execution of robots uploaded in the Web Control Room. The community version provides access to the IQ bot development platforms for a limited number of learning instances and processes.

This is all about the AAE components: Bot Creator, Web Control Room, and Bot Creator and their communication with each other that has been discussed during the architecture and the editions of Automation Anywhere, namely, Enterprise and Community Edition.

Conclusion

In this chapter, we discussed the three components of Automation Anywhere Enterprise software, namely, Bot Creator, which is the development component, Web Control Room, which is the governing or maintenance component, and Bot Runner, which is the execution component. We also learnt about the architecture of the Automation Anywhere Enterprise software.

After completing this chapter, you will have the knowledge about the components of Automation Anywhere Enterprise software, which are Bot Creator, Web Control Room, and Bot Runner, and about their basic functioning. You will also have knowledge about the Automation Anywhere Enterprise architecture and the connection between the three components.

In the next chapter, we will discuss the client application which is used by both, the Bot Creator and Bot Runner to login and the interface and options available to the Bot Creator and Bot Runner in the client application.

Multiple-choice questions

1. **Bots are developed under the _____ component.**

   a. Bot Creator

   b. Bot Runner

   c. Web Control Room

   d. None of the above

2. **Bots are uploaded by the _____ component onto the _____ component:**

   a. Bot Creator; Bot Runner

   b. Bot Runner,; Web Control Room

   c. Bot Creator; Web Control Room

   d. None of the above

3. **Bots are scheduled in the _____ component to be executed on the _____ component.**

   a. Bot Creator; Bot Runner

   b. Web Control Room; Bot Runner

   c. Web Control Room; Bot Creator

   d. None of the above

Answer

1. *a*

2. *c*

3. *b*

CHAPTER 4

Client Application

Introduction

In this chapter, we will deal with the functionality and menu options available in the client application. In this chapter, the differences in the interface of the client application for the Bot Creator and Bot Runner will be discussed. The client application is the interface using which the Bot Creator develops the bot or bot logic, and the Bot Runner uses the client application for the execution of the bots.

Structure

In this chapter, we will discuss the following topics:

- Client application Functionality
- The difference in client application options available for the Bot Creator and Bot Runner

Objectives

After completing this chapter, you should be able to:

- Understand the working of client application
- Understand the availability of options for the Bot Creator and Bot Runner in client application

Client application

In this chapter , we will be working with the Automation Anywhere Enterprise Edition and exploring the functionality available in the Enterprise Edition. It is assumed that to implement the content further discussed in the book, the reader has already installed the Automation Anywhere Enterprise Edition in their machine.

Before we start working with the client application, we need to create two users, first with the Bot Creator license and second, with the Bot Runner license. These users will be created in the Web Control Room, which are referred to as Web CR from hereon. When you open the Web CR for the first time, it will ask you to provide a username and a password. These credentials will be used to create a Web CR user with the Admin rights. In the next step, it will ask for three security questions and answers which will be stored and used in the **Forgot Password** situation. In the next step, it will ask you to select the **Express** or **Manual** mode to save the key to connect with **Credential Vault**. As of now, select **Express Mode**. The difference between the **Express** and **Manual** mode will be discussed later in the book .

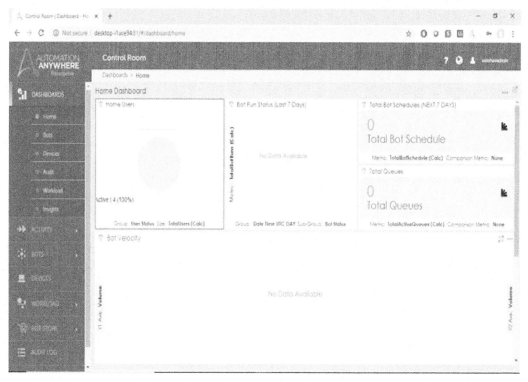

Figure 4.1: Web CR home screen

This is the first screen that opens when you login to the Web CR. The default option that opens is the **Home** option under the **Dashboard** tab. Select the **Administration** tab. Under the **Administration** tab, select **Users** as follows:

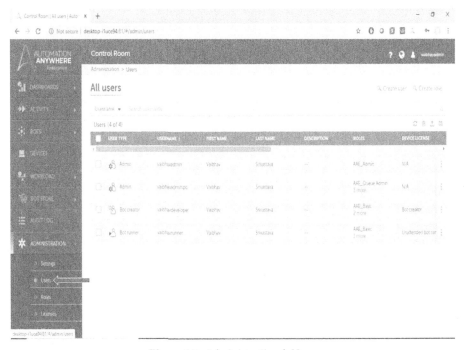

Figure 4.2: *Administration | Users*

Under All users, you will see only one user created with the user type being Admin in your Web CR. Now, on the right-hand top corner, select **Create User** as follows:

Figure 4.3: *Create User option*

For creating the first user, provide the username, password, and email of your choice. The description, first name, and last name fields are optional to be provided. Under the **Roles**, select the **AAE_Basic** and **AAE_MetabotDesigner** roles, and click on the right arrow. Now, move down and under allot **Bot Creator** option under **Allocate license** to the user header. Scroll to the top of the page, and click on the **Create User** button as follows:

Figure 4.4: *Create User screen*

For creating the second user, provide the username, password, and email of your choice. The description, first name, and last name fields are optional to be provided. Under the roles select, the **AAE_Basic** role only and click on the right arrow. Now, move down and under allot **Unattended Bot Runner** option under **Allocate** license to the user header. Scroll to the top of the page, and click on the **Create User** button.

Now, under the **Users** tab, you will see three users with the user type being **Admin,** **Bot Creator**, and **Bot Runner** for each of them. Under the **Administration** tab, select the **Settings** tab and expand the **General** tab. Copy the URL provided under the **Control Room Access** URL heading as follows:

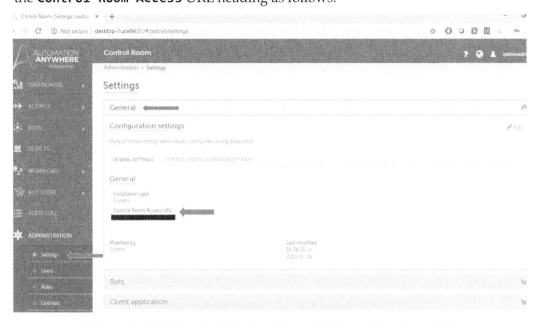

Figure 4.5: Administration | Settings | General | Control Room Access URL

Open the client application now. Provide the URL that you copied under the **Control Room Access** URL under the first textbox. Select the **User Credentials** option and provide the username and password for the user with the **Bot Creator** user type and license and click the **Login** button as follows:

Figure 4.6: Client application first screen

Once you click on the **Login** button, the second screen will open. Either click on the **Automate** button or **Skip** option at the bottom-right of the second screen as follows:

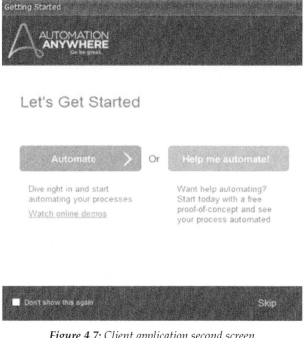

Figure 4.7: Client application second screen

This will lead you to the client application home for the Bot Creator user as follows:

Figure 4.8: Client application bot creator home screen

The robots, henceforth, referred to as bots, in Automation Anywhere are of three types as follows:

- TaskBot
- Metabot
- IQBot

The New option opens up the **Workbench** window which is used to create the Task bots. In the workbench, the task bots are created using the command library or the pre-selected recorder in the client application as follows:

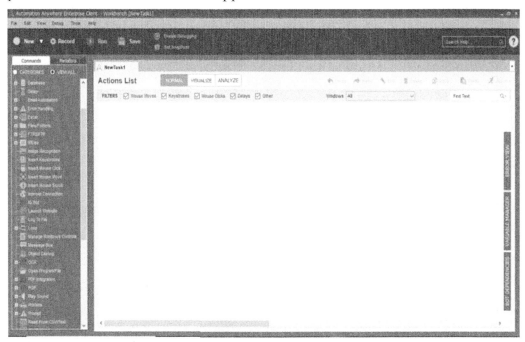

Figure 4.9: Workbench screen

The **Record** option opens up the recorder window through which the steps being performed on the system are captured and saved as a task bot. There are following three types of recorders available in Automation Anywhere:

- Screen recorder
- Web recorder
- Smart recorder

The Run option runs the pre-created and currently selected task bot listed under **My Tasks** table. The **Edit** option opens the pre-created and currently selected task bot listed under **My Tasks** table in the workbench for editing the task bot.

Under **Automate** header on the left side, by default **Tasks** are expanded. The **Tasks** tab lists all the subfolders under the **My Tasks** folder and lists all the task bot on the right under the **My Tasks** table. Following the Tasks tab, you have the **Metabots** tab. The **Metabots** tab lists all the subfolder under the **My Metabots** folder and lists all the task bots on the right under the **My Metabots** table as follows:

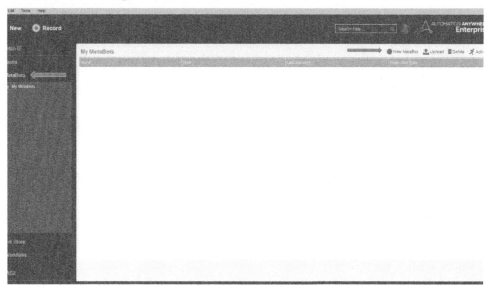

Figure 4.10: Client application Metabot screen

If you click the **New Metabot** button on the top-right corner, it will open **Metabot Designer** which is used to create the metabots as follows:

Figure 4.11: Metabot Designer screen

Following the **Metabots** tab, you have the **Bot Store** tab. The Bot Store is very similar to the App Store of Android or IoS. You can search and download the bots uploaded under different industry domains, or you can search and download for the bots uploaded by different companies. Some of the bots are paid, whereas some are free to download as follows:

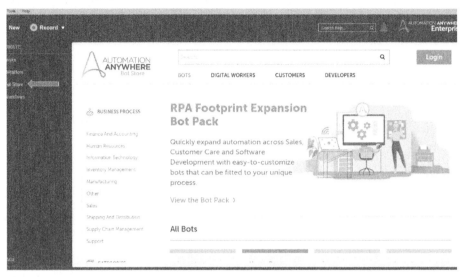

Figure 4.12: Bot Store screen

Following the **Bot Store** tab, you have the **Workflows** tab. The **Workflows** tab lists all the subfolder under the **My Workflow** folder and lists all the workflow on the right under the **My Workflow** table. If you click on the New Workflow button on the top-right corner, you will get the following screen:

Figure 4.13: Client application Workflow screen

It will open **Workflow Designer** which is used to create the workflows that are similar to the flow chart or graphical sequence for the execution of the task bots one after the other as follows:

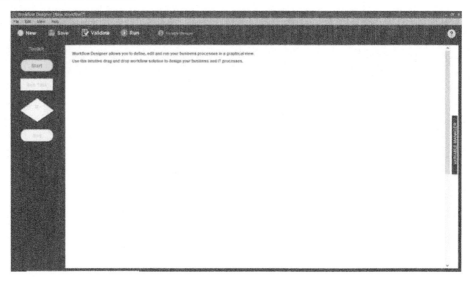

Figure 4.14: Workflow Designer screen

Use the client application login screen and the same steps used for logging in as a Bot Creator to now login as the Bot Runner. The only difference this time would be to provide the username and password of the user created with the Bot Runner user type and license. The home screen of client application for the Bot Runner looks like as follows:

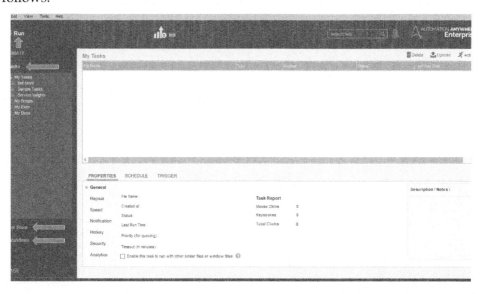

Figure 4.15: Client application bot runner home screen

The Run is the only option available for the Bot Runner meaning that the Bot Runner only has the right to execute the task bot or a workflow. The **New, Record**, and **Edit** options are not available for the Bot Runner. Under the **Automate** tab, only the **Tasks, Bot Store**, and **Workflows** tabs are available. The **Metabots** tab is not available for the Bot Runner.

Conclusion

In this chapter, we discussed the client application and the functionality and options available for the users with the user type and license as the Bot Creator and Bot Runner. The Bot Creator has **New, Recorder, Edit**, and **Run** options available as compared with the Run option available to the Bot Runner. Under the **Automate** tab, the Bot Create has access to the **Tasks, Metabot, Bot Store**, and **Workflow** tabs against the access to the Tasks, Bot Store, and Workflow tabs for the Bot Runner.

After completing this chapter, you have the knowledge about client application and the options available to the Bot Creator and Bot Runner. You also know about the options to access the Workbench, Metabot Designer, Bot Store, and Workflow Designer.

In the next chapter, we will discuss the variables available in Automation Anywhere which are of two types, namely, system and user variables. We will focus on the user variables in the next chapter. The user variables are of five types, namely, *Value, List, Array, Random,* and *Dictionary*.

Multiple-choice questions

1. **The Bot Creator has access to:**

    a. Run

    b. Recorder

    c. New

    d. All of the above

2. **The Bot Creator has access to:**

    a. Tasks

    b. Bot Store

    c. Repository

    d. None of the above

3. **The Bot Runner has access to:**

    a. Run

    b. Recorder

      c.   New

      d.   All of the above

Answer

1. *d*

2. *a, b*

3. *a*

CHAPTER 5
Variables

Introduction

In this chapter , we will deal with the variables and their usage. The variables are of two types, which are the system and user variables. In this chapter, we will focus on the user variables, namely, *value, list, array, random*, and *dictionary* along with the best practices and conventions to use them. These variables are used to store the information during the bot execution.

Structure

In this chapter, we will discuss the following topics:

- **User variables:** *value, list, array, random*, and *dictionary*
- Best practices and convention to use the variables

Objectives

After completing this chapter, you should be able to:

- Understand the variables and their usage
- Understand the convention and best practices to use the variables

Variables

Variable is a memory location that is used to hold some data temporarily. Automation Anywhere primarily has the following two types of variables:

- System
- User

In this chapter, we will be discussing the user variables. The system variables, we will be discussing these throughout the book in the later chapters. The User variables are of five types in Automation Anywhere as shown in the following diagram:

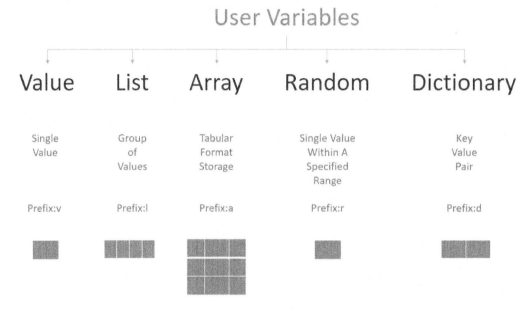

Figure 5.1: *User variables with their format and structure*

As described in the preceding figure , the user variables are of the following five types:

- **Value:** It stores a single data or value and as per the naming convention should have a prefix: v, for example: vMyVar

- **List:** It stores a group of values and as per the naming convention should have a prefix: l, for example: lMyVar

- **Array:** It stores values in a tabular format and as per the naming convention should have a prefix: a, for example: aMyVar

- **Random:** It stores a single data or value within a specified range and as per the naming convention should have a prefix: r, for example: rMyVar

- **Dictionary:** It stores values in a key-value pair and as per the naming convention should have a prefix: d, for example: dMyVar

We will start by creating some exercises to understand how to use each of the user variables. We will start with the value type variables. To start, login to the Client Application with the Bot Creator user credentials, and click on **New** and select **Workbench** to open the workbench screen. Select **Client Application | Bot Creator User Credentials | New | Workbench** as follows:

Figure 5.2: Workbench screen for creating task bot

Value variable

The first task that we will create will take a name input from the user and display it with a welcome message. Click on the **Variable Manager** on the right corner screen and click on **Add** as follows:

Figure 5.3: *Variable Manager | Add*

Once you click the **Add** button, the **Add Variable** window will open. In the **Variable Type** option, take the default selected **Value**. If you click on the dropdown, you can see all the five variable types in the list. In the **Name** option, give the variable name as vName. In the Select option, take the default selected **Value** and click on **Save** button, and click on the **Yes** button in the pop-up window, which says that you are creating a variable with a **Null** value as follows:

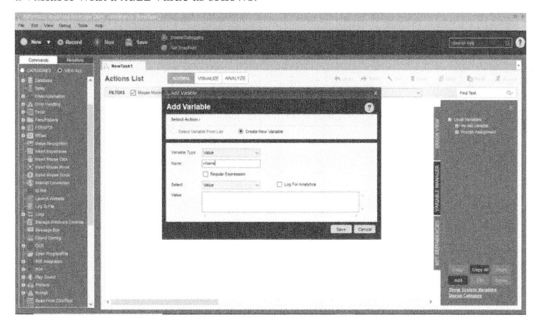

Figure 5.4: *Add vName variable of value type*

This will create a variable **vName**. Now, we will select and move the commands from the **Command Library** on the left to the **New Task** window at the center. You can either drag and drop the commands, or you can put your cursor where you want the command to come and then double click. Under the **Command Library**, you can find the commands by clicking the first letter of the command name or you can select the **Categories** option at the top of the **Command Library** and find the commands under different categories.

It is one of the best practices to have the task logic inside the **Error Handling** block. In the **Command Library**, expand the **Error Handling** command and drag and drop the **Begin Error Handling** subcommand and click on **Save**. The options for the following **Error Handling** command will be discussed later in the book:

Figure 5.5: Begin Error Handling command

To take the name input from the user, expand the **Prompt** command and select the **Prompt For Value** subcommand. In order to get the subcommand at Line 3, drag and drop the **Prompt For Value** subcommand at Line 2. In the **Prompt** window, in the **Select Window** option, select the **Don't write in any window** option. Under the **Provide A Custom Message** option, you can write any message for the user and provide a name in **Please enter a name as of now**. Check the **Assign the value to an existing variable** option and select vName from the dropdown provided just below and click the **Save** button. This step will save the value that the user provides at the run time in the vName variable as follows:

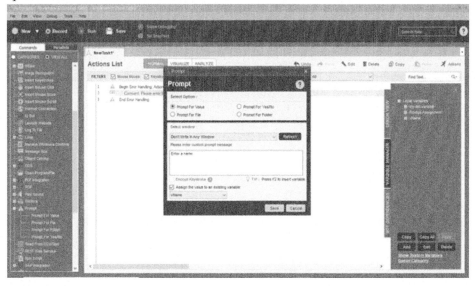

Figure 5.6: Prompt For Value command

The task logic should look like as follows:

Figure 5.7: *Task logic with Begin Error Handling and Prompt For Value command*

The next step would be to show the name input provided by the user through the Prompt command, and for this, use the **Message Box** command. Drag and drop the **Message Box** command at Line 3 or place your cursor on Line 3 and double click on the **Message Box** command in the **Command Library**. You can replace the Automation Anywhere Enterprise Client provided in the first box with the name of your organization to be displayed in the header of the **Message Box** window at the run time. Under the **Please enter a message** to show to the user option, write **Welcome** with space and then press *F2* for the **Insert Variable** window as follows:

Figure 5.8: *Message Box command*

Under the **Insert Variable** window, select vName variable and click on **Insert** button to close the **Insert Variable** window or write the name of the variable preceded and proceeded with $ sign, for example, $vName$ as follows:

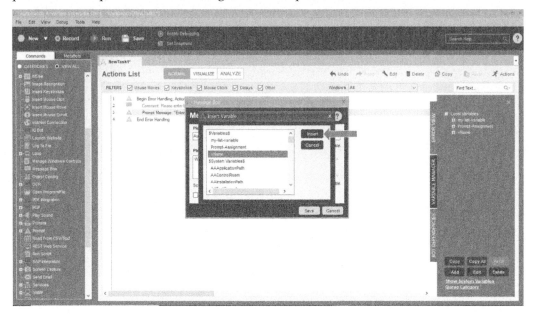

Figure 5.9: Message Box | Insert variable window

Click **Save** on the **Message Box** command as follows:

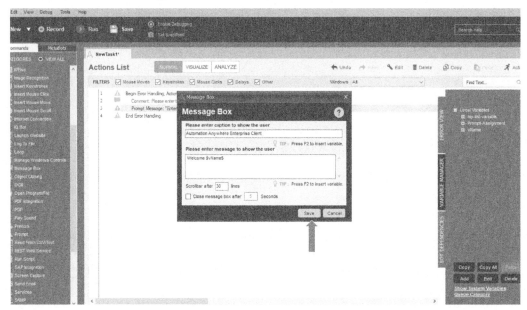

Figure 5.10: Message Box command with a welcome message along with user input

The task logic has been created as follows:

Figure 5.11: *Complete task logic*

Click on the **Save** button on the top and provide a meaningful task name and then click on the **Run** button to execute the bot. As the bot is executed, a **Run Time Window** will appear on the right-bottom of the screen. It will display the name of the bot executing and the line and command of the bot execution. Congratulations on the creation and execution of your first bot.

Conditional construct

The task of the next bot will be to take the two number input from the user, perform a mathematical operation on them, and print the result to the user. Click on the **New** button at the top of the **Workbench** window to create a new task bot. The first step will be to take the **Begin Error Handling** subcommand under the **Error Handling** command and then create the three variables of value type, named vFirstNum, vSecondNum, and vResult, with null value using the Prompt For

Value subcommand under the **Prompt** command, exactly as done for the earlier bot. The task logic should look like as follows:

Figure 5.12: Task logic with two prompt commands along with error handling command

The **Variable Operation** command is used to perform the mathematical operations on the variables. Under the **Specify variable** option, select vResult, and under the Specify value for $Select variable$ option, provide vFirstNum and vSecondNum variable along with the mathematical operation, for example, $vFirstNum$ + $vSecondNum$, using *F2* for the **Insert Variable** window or directly writing it and then click the **Save** button in the **Variable Operation** window as follows:

Figure 5.13: Variable Operation command

The next step is to print the result stored in the vResult variable using the **Message Box** command. The complete task logic should be as follows:

Figure 5.14: Complete task logic.

The task logic has been created. Click on the **Save** button on the top and provide a meaningful task name and then click on the **Run** button to execute the bot.

The task of the next bot will be to take two number input from the user, compare, and find the greater number between the two and print the result to the user. Click on the **New** button at the top of the **Workbench** window to create a new task bot. The first step will be to take **Begin Error Handling** subcommand under the **Error Handling** command and then create the two variables of the value type named vFirstNum and vSecondNum with the null value using the **Prompt For Value** subcommand under the **Prompt** command, exactly as done for the earlier bot. The task logic should look like as follows:

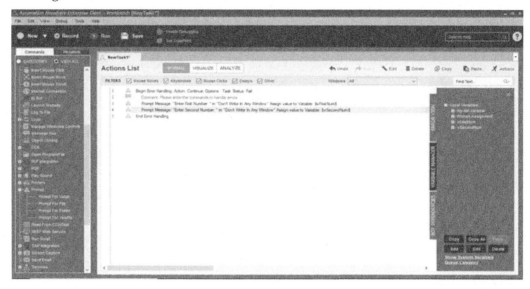

Figure 5.15: *Task logic with two prompt commands along with error handling command*

The **If Else** command is used to compare the values. Expand the **If Else** command, choose the **Variable** subcommand, as we are comparing the variables and click on the **Edit** button as follows:

Figure 5.16: *If-Else command with Variable sub command selected*

In the **Variable** option at the top textbox, select vFirstNum using *F2* through the Insert **Variable** window. In the **Operator** option, select Greater Than(>) from the dropdown list. Select **Variable** in the last option and select vSecondNum again using F2 through the **Insert Variable** window and click on the **Save** button. The Fix option was not used, as the comparison is between the two variables as opposed to a variable is compared with a fixed value, for example, vFirstNum>10 as follows:

Figure 5.17: *If condition with the selections*

The If condition is the opening and End If is the closing of the If Else command. All the conditions will come between If and End If block as follows:

Figure 5.18: *If and End If block*

Use the **Message Box** command at Line 6 and print the message that $vFirstNum$ is greater than $vSecondNum$ as done in the earlier tasks printing the value of the two variables and then click on the **Save** button as follows:

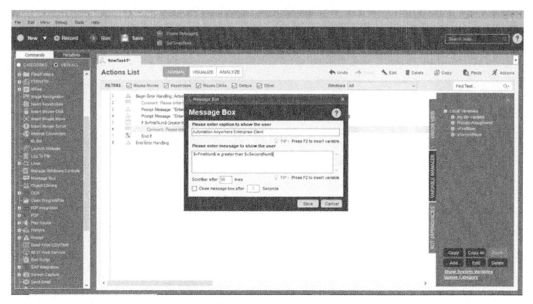

Figure 5.19: *Message box command*

Use the **Else If** subcommand and select **Variable** option and repeat the steps done previously for the If condition with the difference being of the **Operator** selected, which will be **Equal To (=)** and the message in the **Message Box** being that Both numbers are equal as follows:

Figure 5.20: *Else If subcommand with selected options*

The task logic with `If` and `Else If` options have been created as follows:

Figure 5.21: *If and Else If condition blocks with their messages*

Between the `Else If` block and `End If` statements, take the `Else` subcommand. Under the `Else` block, use the **Message Box** command with the message that $vSecondNum$ is greater than $vFirstNum$ as follows:

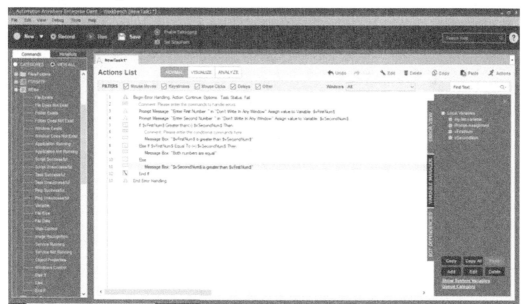

Figure 5.22: *Complete task logic*

The task logic has been created. Click on the **Save** button on the top and provide a meaningful task name and then click on the **Run** button to execute the bot.

Iteration

The task of the next bot will be to take a number of inputs from the user and print the table of the number as a result to the user. Click on the **New** button at the top of the Workbench window to create a new task bot. The first step will be to take the **Begin Error Handling** subcommand under the **Error Handling** command and then create the three variables of the value type named vNum, vCounter with the value being provided as 1 while creating and vResult with null value using the **Prompt For Value** subcommand under the **Prompt** command, exactly as done for the earlier bot:

Figure 5.23: vCounter variable with assigned value 1

The task logic should look like as follows:

Figure 5.24: Task logic with a prompt command along with error handling command

Below the **Prompt** command, select the **Loop** command with the **Times** subcommand. In the **Times** option, provide 10 as the value, as the loop has to be executed 10 times, and now, click on the **Save** button. The **Times** option is used when the exact number of iterations of the steps is fixed as follows:

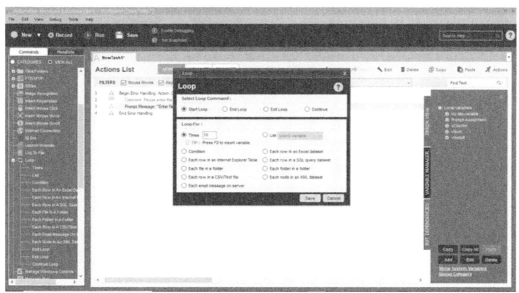

Figure 5.25: Times sub command with value 10

Between the **Start Loop** and **End Loop** block, first, take the **Variable Operation** command with the selection from the dropdown list being vResult on the left side and expression being vNum*vCounter on the right side and click on the **Save** button as follows:

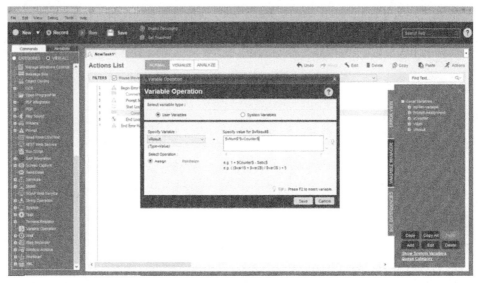

Figure 5.26: Variable Operation command

Next step would be to print the expression vNum * vCounter = vResult as a message using the **Message Box** command. Check the last checkbox to close the message box automatically and change the value to an interval of 2 seconds as follows:

Figure 5.27: Message Box command

The value of the counter needs to be increased by 1 so as to keep the iteration moving forward and table getting printed in the incorrect order. Take the `Variable Operation` command again, and now, select `vCounter` from a dropdown list from the left side, and on the right side, the expression will be `vCounter+1` to increase the value of `vCounter` by 1 in each iteration as follows:

Figure 5.28: *Variable Operation command*

The task logic has been created as follows:

Figure 5.29: *Task logic*

Click on the **Save** button on the top and provide a meaningful task name and then click on the **Run** button to execute the bot. The task will be executed successfully. The value in the message box will be shown one by one. If you want the full table to be stored in a file, then use the **Log To File** command. This will save the file either in a text file or CSV file. As of now, we will use a text file to save the table. After Line 7, which is the **Message Box** command, use the **Log To File** command and in the **Log File** option provide the full path of the text file. Even if, the file is not created, it will be created at the time of execution. In the **Text** option, provide the same expression as given in the **Message Box** command, i.e. vNum * vCounter = vResult and click on the **Save** button as follows:

Figure 5.30: *Log To File command*

Now, again click on the **Save** button on the top and then click on the Run button to execute the bot again and check the full table result in the specified text file as follows:

Figure 5.31: *Complete task logic*

List variable

The task of the next bot will be to see the implementation of the List variable. Click on the **New** button at the top of the **Workbench** window to create a new task bot. The first step will be to take the **Begin Error Handling** subcommand under the **Error Handling** command. Now, create a new variable and in the **Variable Type** option select **List**, provide **Name** as **1MyList**. In the **List Value** option provide the values and keep clicking the **Add To List** button to save the values one after the other in the list variable being created. The values can be heterogeneous or of different types like numbers, characters, decimal values, or alphanumeric values as follows:

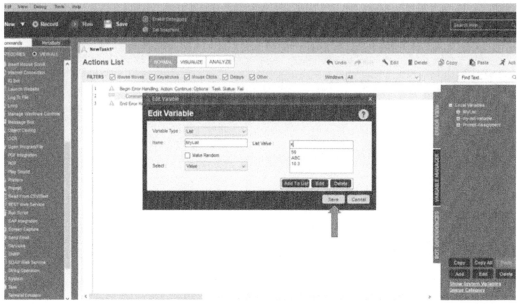

Figure 5.32: List variable

To iterate each value of the list variable one by one, use the **Loop** command and List subcommand. In the **List** option dropdown list, select the list variable that was created for this task which is **1MyList** and click on the **Save** button as follows:

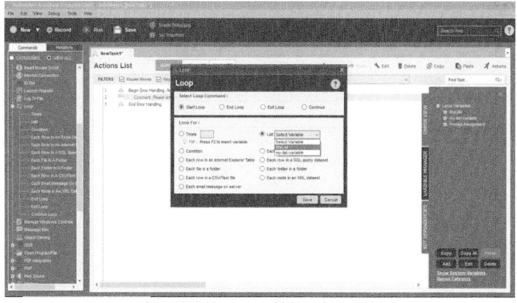

Figure 5.33: Loop command | List subcommand

Between the **Start Loop** and **End Loop** block, take a **Message Box** command and using *F2* select lMyList variable from the **Insert Variable** window as follows:

Figure 5.34: *Message Box command*

The task logic has been created as follows:

Figure 5.35: *Task logic*

Click on the **Save** button on the top and provide a meaningful task name and then click on the **Run** button to execute the bot. The task will be executed successfully. Now, if the values for the list variable are saved in a file and fetched from it, then open the **Variable Manager**, double click on the lMyList variable, and in the **Select** option choose **Read** from the text file as follows:

Figure 5.36: *List Variable | Read from text file option*

Click on the **Browse** button and provide the path of the pre-created text file from which the values for list variable have to be fetched and click on the **Save** button after selecting the file as follows:

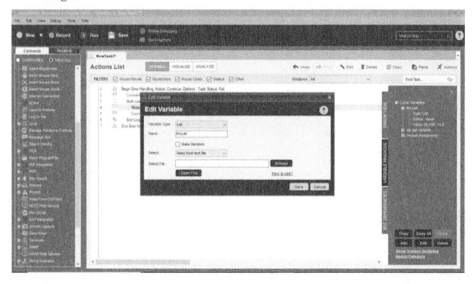

Figure 5.37: *Read from text file | Browse*

The text file should have the same of the variable and then the values separated by a comma as follows:

ListVariable - Notepad
File Edit Format View Help

lMyList=Abhay, Malay, Vinay

Figure 5.38: *A sample Text file with values for list variable*

Now, again click on the **Save** button on the top and then click on the **Run** button to execute the bot again as follows:

Figure 5.39: *Complete task logic*

Array variable

The task of the next bot will be to see the implementation of the Array variable. Click on the **New** button at the top of the **Workbench** window to create a new task bot. The first step will be to take the **Begin Error Handling** subcommand under the **Error Handling** command. Now, create two variables of value type named vRowCounter and vColumnCounter with **Value** being provided 1 and create another variable and in the **Variable Type** option select **Array** and provide **Name** as aMyArray. In the **Rows** option, provide 4 as the value, and in the **Columns** option, provide 3 as the value to create a table of size 4*3 and click on the **Initialize Values** button to open the **Array Values Details** window as follows:

Figure 5.40: Array variable | Initialize Values option

The values can be heterogeneous or of different types like numbers, characters, decimal values, or alphanumeric values. After providing the values, click on the **Save** button as follows:

Figure 5.41: Array Values Details window

In order to access each and every value individually in the array variable, two loops would be required. The first loop will be used to iterate through the rows, and the second loop to iterate through the columns. The task logic should be such that it can handle any number of rows or columns and should be dynamic. This will be achieved using the system variables, namely, ArrayRows and ArrayColumns, as they return the number of rows and columns in the array variable, respectively.

Use the **Loop** command and **Times** subcommand. In the **Times** options, press *F2* and select the ArrayRows variable in the **Insert Variable** window. It would open the **Array Variable Option** window and select aMyArray from the dropdown list as follows:

Figure 5.42: *ArrayRows | Array Variable Option window*

The task logic will look like as follows:

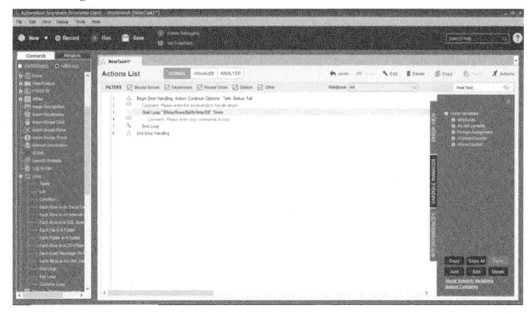

Figure 5.43: Task logic with loop command along with error handling command

Repeat the same steps after Line 4, with the only change being that instead of `ArrayRows` system variable choose `ArrayColumns` variable as follows:

Figure 5.44: Task logic with two loop command along with error handling command

Use the **Message Box** command inside the second loop, press *F2* to open **Insert Variable** window, and select aMyArray variable. This would open the **Array Variable Option** window. In the **Row Value** option, press *F2* and select vRowCounter variable and in the **Column Value** option, press *F2* and select vColumnCounter variable and click the **OK** button as follows:

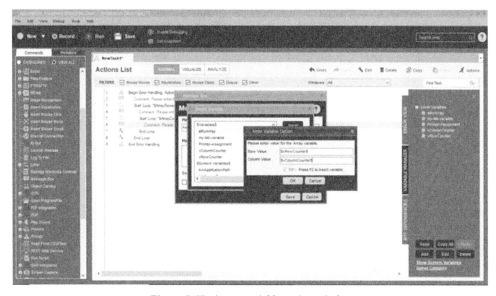

Figure 5.45: *Array variable option window*

Click the **Save** button in the **Message Box** command as follows:

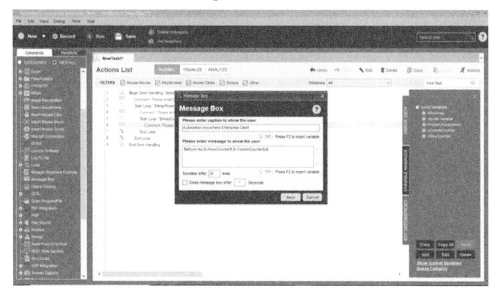

Figure 5.46: *Message Box*

After Line 4, use the **Variable   Operation** command with the variable vColumnCounter selected from the dropdown list on the left side and the expression provided on the right side being 1. After the **Message   Box** command at Line 7, again take the Variable Operation command with the variable selected from the dropdown list on the left side being vColumnCounter and the expression on the right being $vColumnCounter$+1. Repeat the same steps at Line 8 between the two **End Loop** statements, with the only change being that the variable selected from the dropdown list on the left side being vRowCounter and the expression on the right being $vRowCounter$+1 as follows:

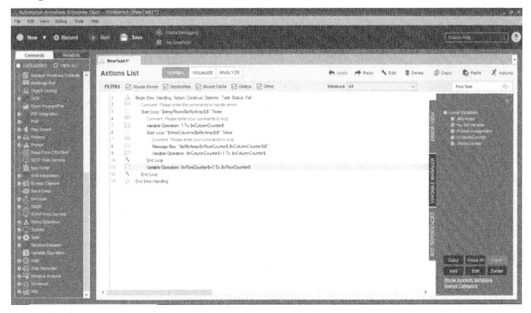

Figure 5.47: *Complete task logic*

The task logic has been created. Click on the **Save** button on the top and provide a meaningful task name and then click on the **Run** button to execute the bot. The task will be executed successfully. Now, if you want the data to be fetched from a text file or excel or a CSV file or database, you can always do that like done in the previous task. The same task logic will handle data from any of the data sources as follows:

```
ArrayVariable - Notepad
File   Edit   Format   View   Help
Name,Age
abc,20
def,24
ghi,28
jkl,32
```

Figure 5.48: *Sample text file*

The sample data in Excel file to be used for `Array` variable is as follows:

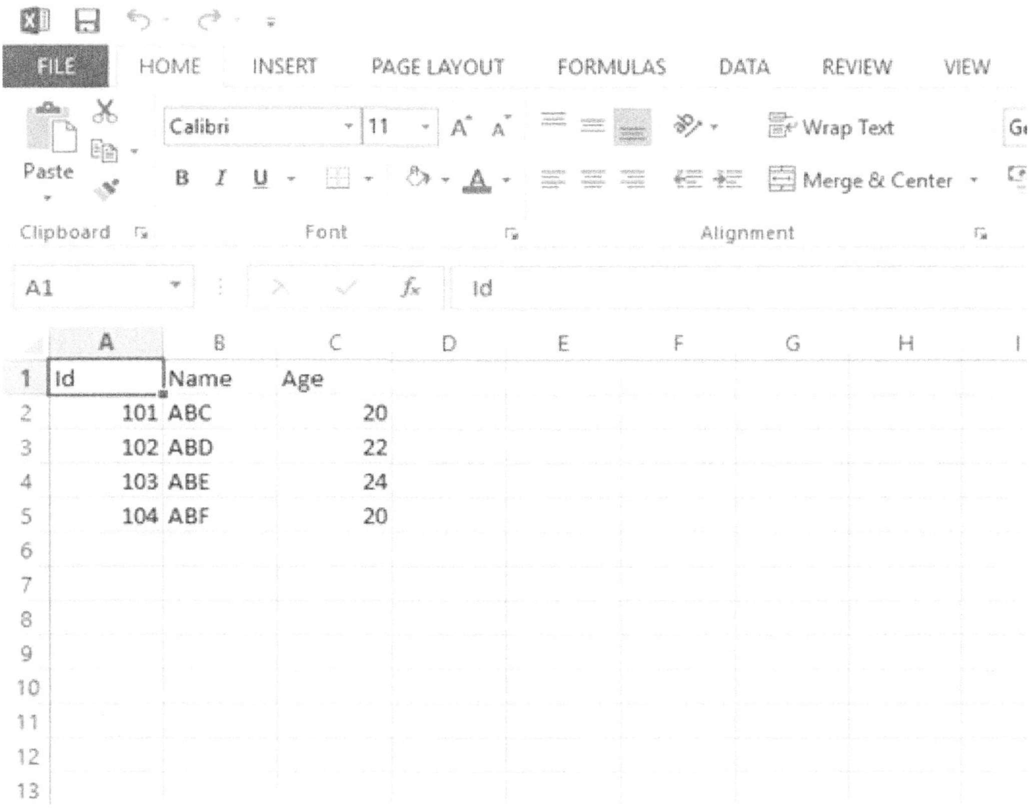

Figure 5.49: Sample excel file

Now, again click on the **Save** button on the top and then click on the **Run** button to execute the bot again.

Random variable

The task of the next bot will be to see the implementation of the Random variable. Click on the **New** button at the top of the **Workbench** window to create a new task bot. The first step will be to take the **Begin Error Handling** subcommand under the **Error Handling** command. Now, create a new variable, and in the **Variable Type** option, select **Random** and provide **Name** as rMyVar. First, let us use the **Random**

String option and provide the **String Length** value as 5 and click on the **Save** button as follows:

Figure 5.50: *Random Variable | String Length option*

In order to check whether the generated values are random strings, either this task is executed multiple times or the same thing is achieved by using a loop. Use the **Loop** command and **Times** subcommand, and the **Times** option value is being provided as 3. Inside the loop, use the **Message Box** command and provide the rMyVar variable using *F2* and **Insert Variable** window as follows:

Figure 5.51: *Complete task logic*

The task logic has been created. Click on the **Save** button on the top and provide a meaningful task name and then click on the **Run** button to execute the bot. The task will be executed successfully. The result will be a generation of the alphanumeric strings of length 5 with random values. If you want that random numbers within a specified range are generated instead of strings, then double click on the rMyVar variable in **Variable Manager** and select the **Random Number – Range** option and provide the range in **From** and **To** options and click the **Save** button as follows:

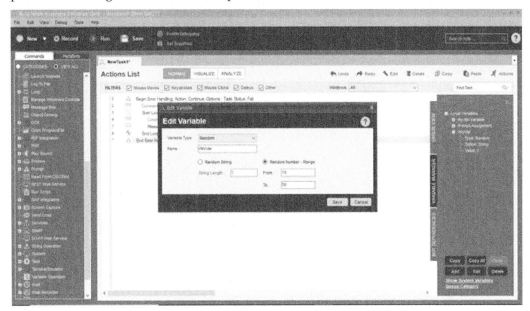

Figure 5.52: *Random number - range option*

Now, again click on the **Save** button on the top and then click on the **Run** button to execute the bot again.

Dictionary variable

The task of the next bot will be to see the implementation of the Dictionary variable. Click on the **New** button at the top of the Workbench window to create a new task bot. The first step will be to take the **Begin Error Handling** subcommand under the **Error Handling** command. Now, create a variable of the value type named vCounter with the value initialized at 1 and create another variable and in the

Variable Type option select **Dictionary**, provide Name as dMyVar, and click on the **Initialize Values** button as follows:

Figure 5.53: Dictionary Variable

Click on the **Add Key** button, provide values in the key-value pair and provide the key as a numeric starting from 1 and increment of 1 for each key and value as a string as follows:

Figure 5.54: Dictionary Variable | Add Key button

After adding the values in the Dictionary variable, use the **Loop** command and **Times** subcommand and give the number of the key value as the value for the **Times** option; for example, if you have given two key-value pairs in the Dictionary variable, provide two in the **Times** option of the loop. Inside the **Loop** command, use the **Message Box** command, press *F2* and in the **Insert Variable** window select the dMyVar variable, which will open **Dictionary Variable Option** window. In the **Dictionary Key** option, press *F2* and select the vCounter variable and click on the **OK** button as follows:

Figure 5.55: *Message Box command | Dictionary Variable Option window*

Click on the **Save** button in the **Message Box as follows**:

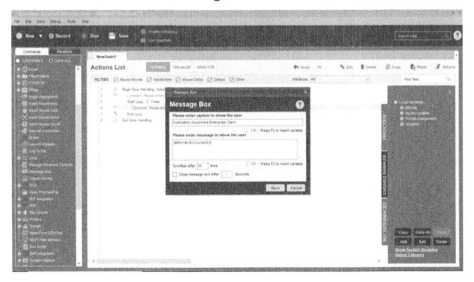

Figure 5.56: *Message Box command*

After the **Message Box** command inside the loop, use the **Variable Operation** command with vCounter being selected from the dropdown list on the left side and the expression on the right side being $vCounter$+1 as follows:

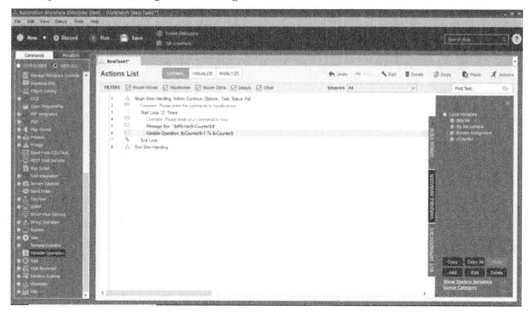

Figure 5.57: Complete task logic

The task logic has been created. Click on the **Save** button on the top and provide a meaningful task name and then click on the **Run** button to execute the bot. The task will be executed successfully. The value against each key will be displayed as a result.

Conclusion

In this chapter, we discussed the variables that are primarily of two types, namely, system and user, and focused on user variables and their implementation. The user variables are of five types, namely, value, list, array, random, and dictionary.

You have now learnt to use the different types of variables for storing values. The value type variable stores a single value or data. The list type variable stores a group of values. The array type variable stores values in a tabular format. The random variable stores a single value within a specified range or generates a random string of the provided string length. The dictionary variable stores the values in a key-value pair format. We also saw the usage of multiple commands like **Prompt, Message Box, Variable Operation**, and the implementation of conditions using the If Else command, iterations through the Loop command.

In the next chapter, we will automate a few industry standard use cases, which will be Excel Data Processing, Web Data Extractor, Stock Price Infuser, Database Data Extractor, and Invoice Processing.

Multiple choice questions

1. **Choose the correct user variables:**

   a. String

   b. List

   c. Array

   d. Integer

2. **Which variable stores value in a tabular format:**

   a. List

   b. Dictionary

   c. Array

   d. None of the above

3. **Which variable stores the value in a key-value format:**

   a. List

   b. Dictionary

   c. Array

   d. None of the above

4. **Which command is used to perform the mathematical operations on the numeric values?**

   a. Prompt

   b. Message Box

   c. Variable Operation

   d. None of the above

Answer

1. *b, c*

2. *c*

3. *b*

4. *c*

CHAPTER 6
Use Cases

Introduction

In the previous chapter, we learned about how to write alphabets and form words in reference to RPA. In this chapter, we will learn to form sentences and paragraphs and automate a lot of day-to-day repetitive processes. In this chapter, we will automate a few industry-standard use cases involving commands like Excel, database, object cloning, email, PDF, and more. The use cases that will be discussed in this chapter will be Excel data processing, web data extractor, stock price infuser, database data extractor, and invoice processing.

Structure

In this chapter, we will discuss the following topics:

- Use cases
- Usage of multiple commands together to create an end-to-end process automation

Objectives

After completing this chapter, you should be able to:

- Understand how to use multiple commands together
- Understand the automation of some industry-standard processes

Use cases

In the previous chapter, we learnt the basics of variables and how to use them in conjunction with commands to create very basic automation. This could be compared with learning alphabets and forming words. This chapter would be to build on the previous learning and take it forward to automate end-to-end processes. It would be equivalent to learning to form sentences and write paragraphs. In this chapter, we will be implementing the following use cases:

- Excel data processing
- Web data extractor
- Stock price infuser
- Database data extractor
- Invoice processing

Excel data processing

Let us start with the first use case. The first use case is Excel data processing. This is a three-step process automation. The steps are as follows: extracting data from an Excel sheet, writing the extracted data into a row by row form into designated fields, and submitting the data into the database. Let us start with the first step. The following is a snapshot of the data that is being stored in the Excel sheet:

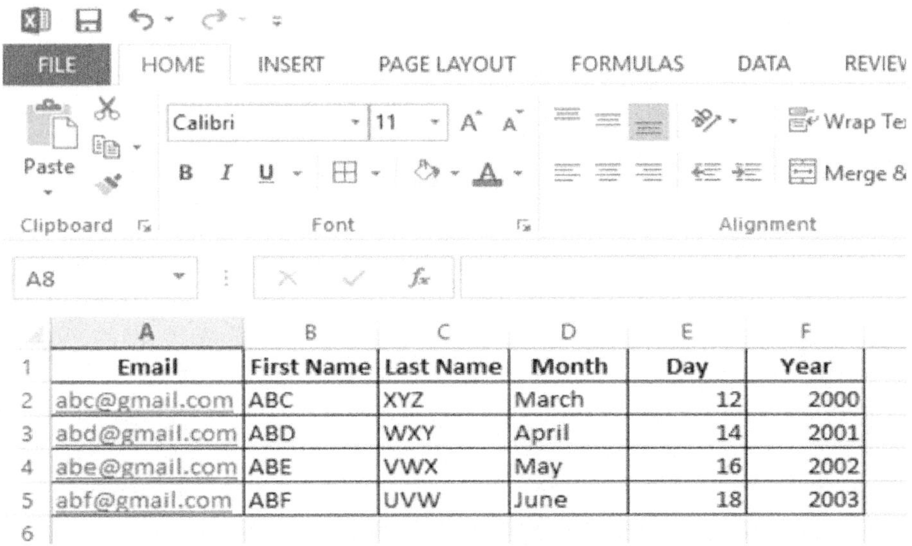

Figure 6.1: Sample Excel Data

You can have any sample data with any number of columns. The Excel sheet that is being used in the book has seven columns and almost a thousand rows. Let us start with the task creation. Open **Workbench** and click on the **New** button at the top of the **Workbench** window to create a new task bot. The first step will be to take the **Begin Error Handling** subcommand under the **Error Handling** command. The task logic should look like as follows till here:

Figure 6.2: Task logic with error handling command

Now, the first step in the automation would be to open the Excel sheet from which the data has to be extracted. Use the **Excel** command and the **Open Spreadsheet** subcommand as follows:

Figure 6.3: Excel command | Open Spreadsheet subcommand

Click on the black button with three dots to provide the path of the Excel sheet from which the data has to be extracted. The data would be extracted from Sheet 1 by default. If the data has to be extracted from any other sheet of the Excel file like Sheet 3 or Sheet 10, then provide the name of the sheet by checking the Specific Sheet Name checkbox and providing the original name of the sheet. In this example, Sheet 1 is being used, and, thus, there is no need to use the aforementioned option. Whenever the data is being extracted and you don't want the first row or column names to be processed, then check the **Contains Header** checkbox. Click the **Save** button. The next step is to extract the data from all the rows that contain data. Use the **Excel** command, **Get Cells** subcommand, and **Get All Cells** option and click on the **Save** button as follows:

Figure 6.4: Excel command | Get Cells subcommand

The **Get Cells** subcommand provides three options to extract data. The three options are **Get Single Cell** to extract the data from a particular cell, for example, **B16**, **Get Multiple Cells** to extract the data of the cells in the provided range, for example, A10: B20, and **Get All Cells** to extract the data of all the cells that have data filled in them.

The next step would be to open the web application in which the data is to be propagated. Use the **Web Recorder** command and the **Open Browser** subcommand and pass the URL for the application and click on the **Save** button as follows:

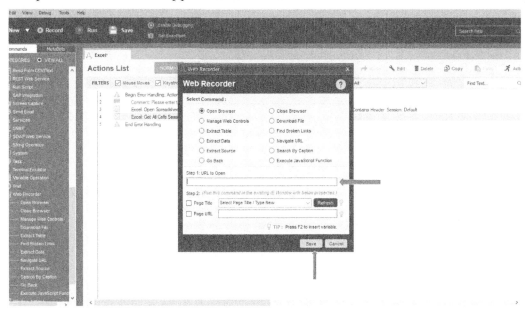

Figure 6.5: *Web Recorder command | Open Browser subcommand*

The application during the execution will be opened in **Internet Explorer**. Open the web application in Internet Explorer separately for further task development as follows:

r.com/form-5282659/my-form   ~ C Search...

Data Submission

Email

First Name

Last Name

Month	Day	Year
January	1	2000

SUBMIT FORM

Figure 6.6: *Sample Web Application*

Now, to access the data row by row, use the **Loop** command and the **Each Row In An Excel Dataset** subcommand and click on the **Save** button as follows:

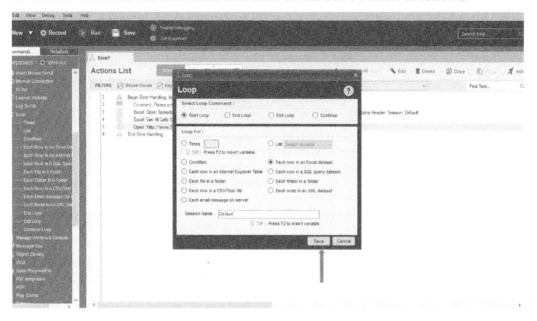

Figure 6.7: *Loop command | Each Row In An Excel Dataset subcommand*

The task logic will look like as follows:

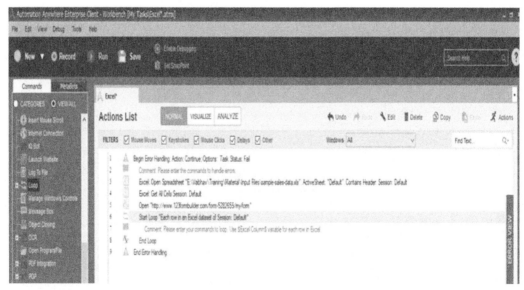

Figure 6.8: *Task logic with the loop command*

The data extracted from the Excel sheet is being stored in the clipboard or at a temporary memory location. The column's value of this data can be accessed using the variable **Excel Column** along with either column numbers starting with 1 for the first column or column names exactly matching the names in the Excel sheet. A variable name for accessing the column values is always mentioned in the comment inside the **Loop** command. The next step is to propagate the first column value into the first textbox of the web application form. Use **Object Cloning** inside the loop to capture the text box and pass the value in the box. In the **Select Window** option, select the combination of the title of the tab and the application. In this scenario, title of the tab is **My Form** and the application is **Internet Explorer**. So, the **Select Window** selection option would be **My Form - Internet Explorer**. Click on the **Capture** button and keep it pressed. It will open the web application form, and then, drag the cursor to the text box to be captured as follows:

Figure 6.9: *Object Cloning command*

Release the mouse button when a red outline appears around the text box gesturing that the properties of the textbox have been captured to identify the text box at the time of execution as follows:

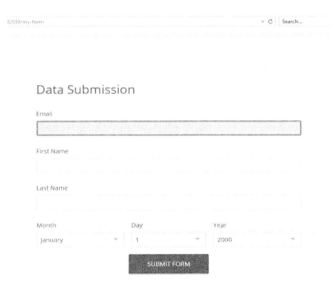

Figure 6.10: Object Cloning command capturing the text box

Check whether the object properties have been captured under the **Object Details** section as follows:

Figure 6.11: Object Cloning command after capturing of the text box and properties captured

Under the **Select Action** option, select **Set Text**. In the **Text To Set** option, press *F2* as follows:

Figure 6.12: *Object Cloning command | Select Action option*

In the **Insert Variable** window, select **Excel Column** and click on the Insert button, as it will open the **Excel Column Option** window as follows:

Figure 6.13: *Object Cloning command | Text To Set option | Insert Variable window*

In the **Excel Column Option** window, pass either 1 or the first column header value of the Excel sheet there and click on the **OK** button as follows:

Figure 6.14: *Object Cloning command | Text To Set option | Insert Variable window | Excel Column Option window*

In the **Object Cloning** window, click on the **Save** button as follows:

Figure 6.15: *Object Cloning command with all the filling options*

Repeat the same process for the second and the third text box. The process to propagate value into the dropdown list is a two-step process. First, use the **Variable Operation** command and on the left side selection, select the **Prompt-Assignment** variable and on the right side, use *F2* and provide **Excel Column(4)** or **Excel Column(Month)** as value repeating the steps in earlier command and click on the **Save** button as follows:

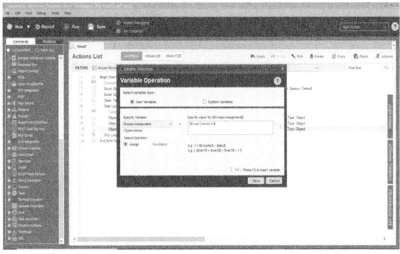

Figure 6.16: Variable Operation command

The second step is to use the **Object Cloning** command, and repeat the same steps as for the text box with the difference being in the **Select Action** option. Select the **Select Item By Text** option, and in the **Item to be Selected** option, pass the **Prompt-Assignment** variable using *F2* through the **Insert Variable** window and click on the **Save** button. Repeat the same steps for the other two dropdown lists as follows:

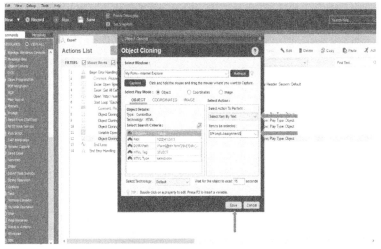

Figure 6.17: Object Cloning command

The task logic will look like as follows:

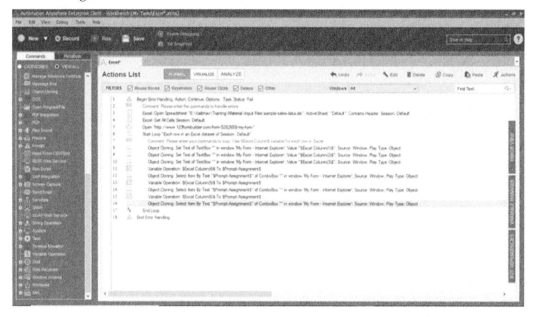

Figure 6.18: Task logic

Click on the **Save** button on the top and provide a meaningful task name and then click on the **Run** button to execute the bot and check the correct execution of the task logic till here.

The last step is to submit the data into the database. There are two ways to do this step. First and the normally used will be to capture the **Submit** button at the bottom of the web application form using the **Object Cloning** command and in the **Select Action** option select **Click**. This way will be used when you are automating your day-to-day organization applications, as the submit button in the application will already have the code in the backend to transfer the data into the database directly. The second way can be used if you are practicing at home or you want to write the database query to submit the data, thus, controlling the flow of the data into the database.

Use the **Database** command and **Connect** subcommand at Line 6 just before the start of the **Loop** command to establish the connection with the database server in which you want to submit the data of the Excel sheet. Click on the button with *three dots* under the **Connection String** option as follows:

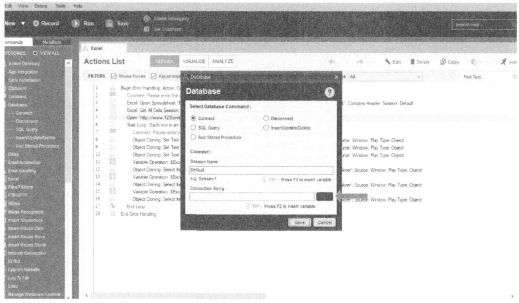

Figure 6.19: *Database command | Connect subcommand*

Under the **Data Link Properties** window and **Provider** tab, select the provider or connector for the database server you are using. The database server used for this task is the SQL server, so the provider selected is **Microsoft OLE DB Provider for SQL Server** as follows:

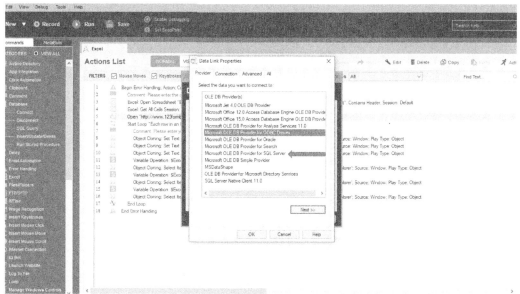

Figure 6.20: *Database command | Connect sub command | Data Link Properties window | Provider tab*

Select the provider according to your database server and click on the **Next** button. Under the **Data Link Properties** window and **Connection** tab, provide the settings for the connection to be established with the database server. Provide the database server name under the **Select or enter a server name** option; after which, provide the login credentials for the database server; then select the database under the **Select the database on the server** option; then click on **Test Connection** button, and if the connection is successful, then click on the **OK** button as follows:

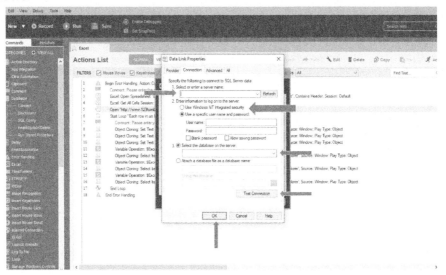

Figure 6.21: *Database command | Connect sub command | Data Link Properties window | Connection tab*

When the connection string is propagated in the **Database** command window, click on the **Save** button as follows:

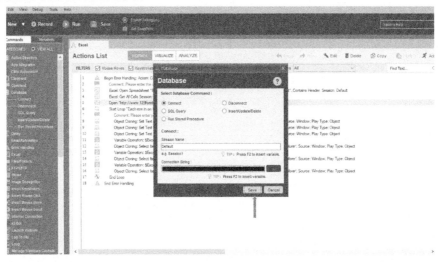

Figure 6.22: *Database command | Connect subcommand with the connection string*

Create a table in the database that will have the structure provided as follows:

Column Name	Data Type	Allow Nulls
Email	varchar(500)	☑
FirstName	varchar(500)	☑
LastName	varchar(500)	☑
Month	varchar(20)	☑
Day	int	☑
Year	int	☑
		☐

Figure 6.23: Table structure with the table name being T1

Just before the **End Loop** statement at Line 18, use the **Database** command and **Insert/ Update/Delete** subcommand. Under the **Enter Insert/Update/Delete** statement, provide the following SQL query and click on the **Save** button:

```
Insert into T1 values ('Excel Column(1)', 'Excel Column(2)', 'Excel Column(3)', 'Excel Column(4)', Excel Column(5), Excel Column(6))
```

In the following figure, the first four columns are inside the ' ' symbol, as they are of varchar type, and the last two columns being of int type do not require values to be passed inside the ' ' symbol, as it is the syntax of the SQL query:

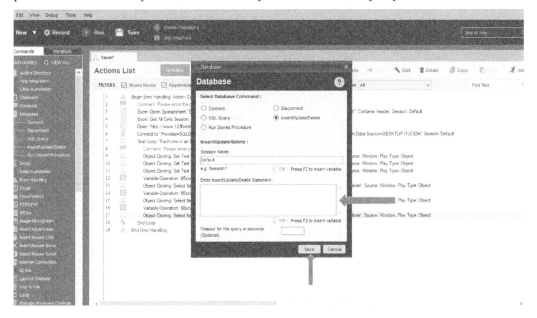

Figure 6.24: Database command | Insert/Update/Delete sub command

After the **End Loop** statement at Line 20, use the **Database** command and **Disconnect** subcommand to disconnect from the database after the submission of the data into the database. At Line 21, use the **Web Recorder** command and **Close Browser** command to close the web application form in the **Internet Explorer**. At Line 22, use the **Excel** command and **Close Spreadsheet** subcommand to close the Excel sheet. Select the **Do not save changes** checkbox to suppress the pop-up message that requires a manual intervention to close the file with or without saving the changes. If you select this checkbox, the manual intervention required is removed as follows:

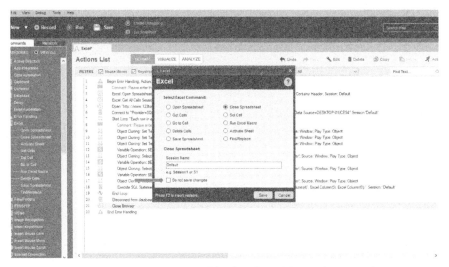

Figure 6.25: *Excel command | Close Spreadsheet subcommand*

The complete task logic will look like as follows:

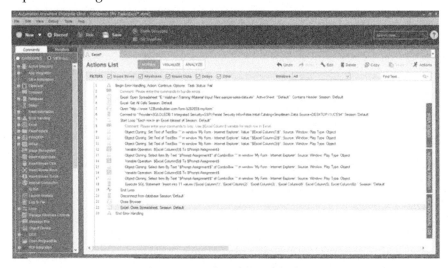

Figure 6.26: *Complete task logic*

Now, again click on the **Save** button on the top and then, click on the **Run** button to execute the bot again and check the full table result in the specified database.

Web data extractor

The next use case is the web data extractor. This is a two-step process automation. The steps are as follows: extracting data from the web application and writing the extracted data into an Excel sheet. Let us start with the task creation. Open **Workbench**. Click on the New button at the top of the **Workbench** window to create a new task bot. The first step will be to take the **Begin Error Handling** subcommand under the **Error Handling** command. The task logic should look like as follows till here:

Figure 6.27: Task logic with error handling command

Now, the first step in the automation would be to open the web application from which the data has to be extracted. Use the **Web Recorder** command and **Extract Table** subcommand and provide the URL **https://old.nasdaq.com** under Step 1 and click on the **Launch** button as follows:

Figure 6.28: Web Recorder command | Extract Table subcommand

Once the website is opened and **Capture Table** is enabled, click on the **Capture Table** button as follows:

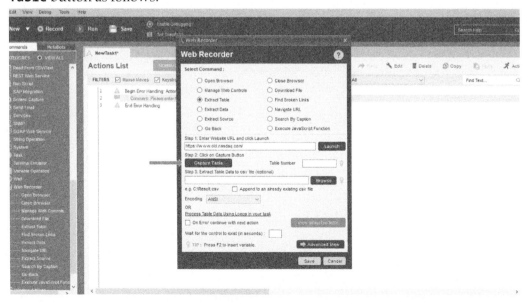

Figure 6.29: Web Recorder command | Extract Table subcommand with Capture Table button enabled

Take the cursor on the data to be captured which is the table under **Stock Market Overview** and wait till the green border appears around the table. The green border implies that the table has been captured as follows:

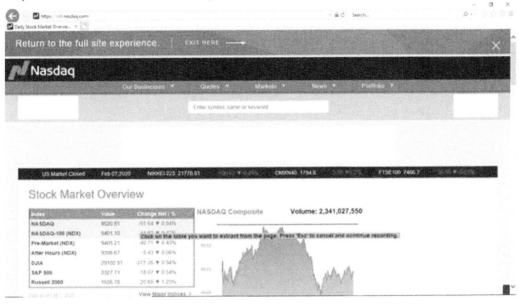

Figure 6.30: *Capture Table button click | green border around the table to be captured*

Once the table is captured, the **Table Number** option will have an automatically filled value and the **View Extracted Table** button will be enabled, and now, click on the **Save** button as follows:

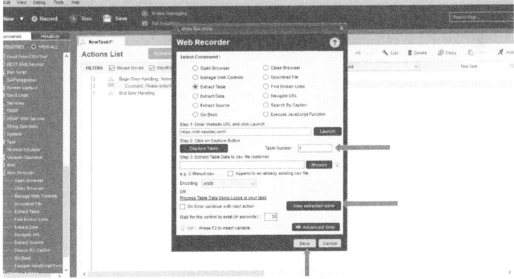

Figure 6.31: *Web Recorder command | Extract Table subcommand with pre-filled Table Number value and View Captured Table button enabled*

Use the Excel command and **Open Spreadsheet** command to open a pre-created Excel file as done in the previous task. Select the **Do not select the Contains Header** option as the data is being written into the Excel sheet. Now, use the Excel command and **Go To Cell** subcommand, and in the **Specific Cell** option, provide **A1**, as the writing of the data has to start from the first cell and then, click on the **Save** button as follows:

Figure 6.32: Excel command | Go To Cell subcommand

Use the **Loop** command and **Each Row In An Internet Explorer Table** subcommand and click on the **Save** button. The variable to iterate through the column values will be **Table Column** and will be used as in the earlier task as follows:

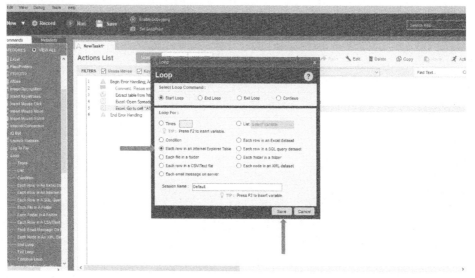

Figure 6.33: Loop command | Each Row in an Internet Explorer table subcommand

Inside the loop, use the Excel command and **Set Cell** subcommand and under the **Cell Value** option provide **Table Column(1)** through **Insert Variable** window using *F2* and then, click on the **Save** button as follows:

Figure 6.34: Excel command | Set Cell subcommand

The first column data has been written into the first cell which is **A1**. Now, to write the second column data into **B1**, the cursor has to move from **A1** to **B1** by making **B1** as the active cell. Use the **Excel** command and **Go To Cell** subcommand and select **One Cell** to right option to achieve the same and then, click on the **Save** button as follows:

Figure 6.35: Excel command | Go To Cell subcommand

Repeat the same process to write the **Table Column(2)** value into **B1** and move to **C1** and write the **Table Column(3)** value into C1. The data has been written in the first row. The active cell should be **A2** now to write the data into the second row. After writing the value into **C1**, use the **Excel** command and **Go To Cell** subcommand and **One cell** below option and click on the **Save** button as follows:

Figure 6.36: Excel command | Go To Cell sub command | One cell below option

The active cell is **C2** now, as the cursor moved from **C1** to **C2**. Again, use the Excel command and **Go To Cell** subcommand and **Beginning of the row** option and click on the **Save** button to move the cursor from **C2** to **A2**, making **A2** as the active cell as follows:

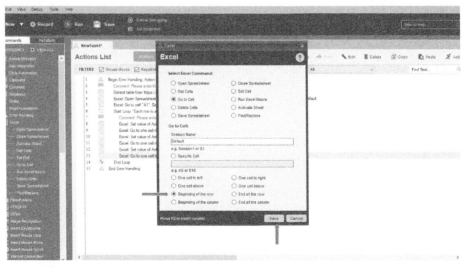

Figure 6.37: Excel command | Go To Cell subcommand | Beginning of the row option

After the **End Loop** statement at Line 15, use the Excel command and **Save Spreadsheet** subcommand to save the data in the Excel sheet. Use the Excel command and **Close Spreadsheet** subcommand to close the Excel sheet. Use the **Web Recorder** command and **Close Browser** subcommand to close the browser.

Click on the **Save** button on the top and provide a meaningful task name and then click on the **Run** button to execute the bot and check the result in the specified Excel file as follows:

Figure 6.38: Complete task logic

Stock price infuser

The next use case is the stock price infuser. This use case will read the company's name one by one from the Excel sheet, then extract its share price from the website, and write the share price in the same Excel file as follows:

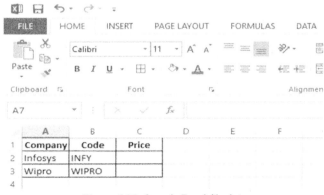

Figure 6.39: Sample Excel file data

Let us start with the task creation. Open **Workbench**. Click on the **New** button at the top of the **Workbench** window to create a new task bot. The first step will be to take the **Begin Error Handling** subcommand under the **Error Handling** command and then create a three-user variable of value type named **vSharePrice** with the value being provided 2 and **vCompanyURL** and **vSharePrice** with null value. The task logic should look like as follows till here:

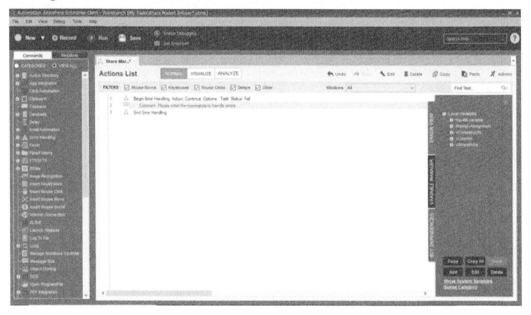

Figure 6.40: Task logic with error handling command

Use the **Excel** command and **Open Spreadsheet** subcommand to open the Excel sheet as done in an earlier task. Use the **Excel** command and **Get Cells** subcommand and **Get All Cells** option to extract all the data from the Excel sheet as done in an earlier task. Use the **Loop** command and **Each Row In An Excel Dataset** subcommand as done in an earlier task. The variable used for this loop again will be **Excel Column** as done in an earlier task. Inside the loop, take a **Variable Operation** command, and on the left side provide the variable vCompanyURL, and on the right, side provide **https://www1.nseindia.com/live_market/dynaContent/ live_watch/get_quote/GetQuote.jsp?symbol=$Excel Column(2)$** through the **Insert Variable** window using F2 to create the URL for extracting the share price. Use the **Web Recorder** command and **Open Browser** subcommand to open the website and under Step 1 provide vCompanyURL variable through the **Insert Variable** window using *F2* and click on the **Save** button as follows:

Figure 6.41: Excel command | Open Browser subcommand

Use the **Object Cloning** command. Under the **Select Window** option, select **NSE - National Stock Exchange of India Ltd. - Internet Explorer** option and click on the **Capture** button to capture the share price as done in the earlier task as follows:

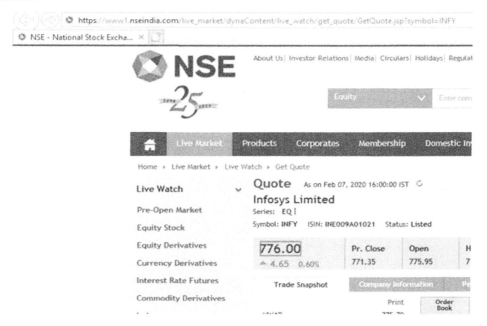

Figure 6.42: Share price value to be extracted

Once the share price has been captured, under **Select action to perform** option, select the **Get Property** option, under the **Select Property** option, select **HTML Inner Text**, and under the **Assign to Variable** option, select the vSharePrice variable and click on the **Save** button as follows:

Figure 6.43: Object Cloning command with all the selected options

Use the **Excel** command and **Set Cell** subcommand. Select the **Specific Cell** option and write C$vCounter$, as it will move the cursor to the **C2** cell as the vCounter variable has initial value 2. Under the **Cell Value** option, provide the vSharePrice variable through the Insert Variable window using *F2* and click on the **Save** button as follows:

Figure 6.44: Excel command | Set Cell subcommand

Use the **Variable Operation** command, and on the left side, provide the vCounter variable, and on the right side, provide the expression **$vCounter$+1** to increase the value of the vCounter variable by 1. Use the **Web Recorder** command and **Close Browser** subcommand to close the browser. After the **End Loop** statement, use the Excel command and **Save Spreadsheet** subcommand to save the Excel sheet. Use the Excel command and **Close Spreadsheet** subcommand to close the spreadsheet as follows:

Figure 6.45: Complete task logic

Click on the **Save** button on the top and provide a meaningful task name, and then, click on the **Run** button to execute the bot and check the result in the Excel file.

Database data extractor

The next use case is the database data extractor. This use case will extract the data stored in the database table and write the extracted in a CSV file as follows:

Column Name	Data Type	Allow Nulls
Email	varchar(500)	☑
FirstName	varchar(500)	☑
LastName	varchar(500)	☑
Month	varchar(20)	☑
Day	int	☑
Year	int	☑

Figure 6.46: Table structure with the table name being T1

The data stored in the database table **T1** is as follows:

Figure 6.47: Sample database table data the table name being T1

Let us start with the task creation. Open **Workbench**. Click on the **New** button at the top of the **Workbench** window to create a new task bot. The first step will be to take the **Begin Error Handling** subcommand under the **Error Handling** command. The task logic should look like as follows till here:

Figure 6.48: Task logic with error handling command

Use the **Database** command and **Connect** subcommand to connect to the database server as done in an earlier task. Use the **Database** command and **SQL Query** subcommand to write the query to extract the data from the database table named **T1**. Under the **Enter Select** statement, provide the following SQL query and click on the **Save** button as follows:

```
Select * from T1
```

Figure 6.49: *Database command | SQL Query subcommand*

Use the **Loop** command and **Each Row** in the SQL query dataset subcommand, and the variable to iterate through the column values for this loop is **Dataset Column**. Inside the loop command, use the **Log To File** command and under the **Log File** option, provide the path of the pre-created file or the file to be created at runtime using the **Browse** button. Under the **Text** option, provide the following expression: $Dataset Column(1)$, $Dataset Column(2)$, $Dataset Column(3)$, $Dataset Column(4)$, $Dataset Column(5)$, $Dataset Column(6)$, and then, click on the **Save** button as follows:

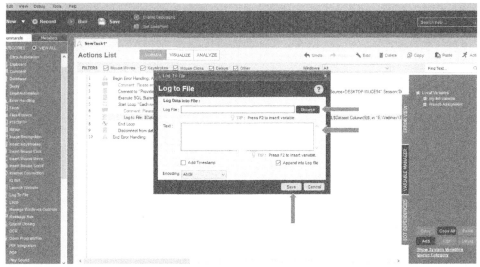

Figure 6.50: *Log To File command*

After the **End Loop** statement, use the **Database** command and **Disconnect** subcommand to disconnect from the database server as follows:

Figure 6.51: Complete task logic

Click on the **Save** button on the top and provide a meaningful task name, and then, click on the **Run** button to execute the bot and check the result in the CSV file.

Invoice processing

Let us start with the last use case. The use case is invoice processing. This is a four-step process automation. The steps are as follows: downloading invoices from the email, extracting values from invoices, writing the extracted data into an Excel sheet, and sending an email with the Excel sheet as an attachment. The following is the snapshot of the sample invoices:

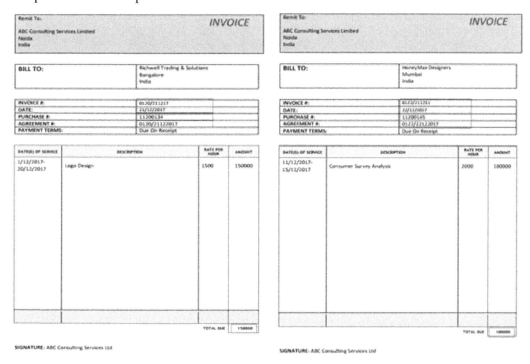

Figure 6.52: Sample Invoices: Invoice1.pdf & Invoice2.pdf

The fields that will be extracted from invoices are **Invoice Number, Date, Purchase Number, Agreement Number**, and **Amount**. These fields have been marked with a red border in the previous sample invoices. Let us start with the task creation. **Open Workbench**. Click on the **New** button at the top of the **Workbench** window to create a new task bot. The first step will be to take the **Begin Error Handling** subcommand under the **Error Handling** command, and then, create a five user variable of value type named vInvoiceNo, vDate, vPurchaseNo, vAgreementNo, and vAmount with the null value. The task logic should look like as follows till here:

Figure 6.53: *Task logic with error handling command*

Keep the invoices in a separate folder that will have only the invoices and no other file. The task creation will be started with the second step, and then, implement the third and fourth step, and the first step will be implemented at the last in the task logic creation. Use the **Excel** command and **Open Spreadsheet** subcommand to open a pre-created blank Excel file. Use the **Excel** command and **Go To Cell** subcommand, and in the **Specific Cell** option, mention **A1**. Use the **Loop** command and **Each File In A Folder** subcommand and provide the path of the folder in which invoices have been kept under the **Select Folder** option by clicking the **Browse** button, and then, click on the **Save** button as follows:

Figure 6.54: *Loop command | Each File In A Folder subcommand*

Use the **PDF Integration** command and **Extract Form Fields** subcommand, and under **PDF Name** option, provide the path of Invoice1.pdf file and provide a password if the file is password protected under the **Password(s)** option, and then, click on the **Add** button under the **Inserted Fields** option as follows:

Figure 6.55: *PDF Integration command | Extract Form Fields subcommand*

This will open the Invoice.pdf file in the PDF viewer, and the extraction of the data will be done here. If you want, you can zoom in to mark the value in the area to be extracted as follows:

Figure 6.56: *Invoice1.pdf file opened in PDF Viewer*

Mark around the area around the data that you want to capture and a blue border will appear around it. Mark a longer area, as it will allow the longer values also to be captured if provided in other invoices as follows:

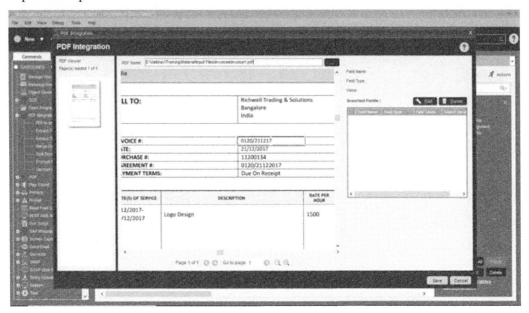

Figure 6.57: Marking of the area for the value to be captured with the blue border

Once the blue border appears, right-click inside the blue border and click on the **Add Field** button as follows:

Figure 6.58: Add Field button

After clicking on the **Add Field** button, the **Extract Text** window will appear. Check that the correct value has been extracted under the **Value** option, provide a unique name under **Field Name** option, and the **Variable** option will provide the user-created variable name corresponding to the extracted data. At this instance, the invoice number value has been extracted, so under the **Variable** option, provide the vInvoiceNo variable, and then, click on the **OK** button as follows:

Figure 6.59: Extract text window

As the field get added, it will be displayed under the **Inserted Fields** panel on the right-side corner. Repeat the steps to extract the values from the invoice, and then, click on the **Save** button as follows:

Figure 6.60: Extract text window with the captured fields

Under the **PDF Name** option, reach to the end of the file path that will be in a similar format, `FullFilePath\Invoice1.pdf`. Remove only `Invoice1` and press *F2* at the same spot and insert the `FileName` variable through the **Insert Variable** window so that during the execution each of the invoices in the folder can be processed. The file path under the **PDF Name** option should resemble `FullFilePath\$FileName$.pdf` as follows:

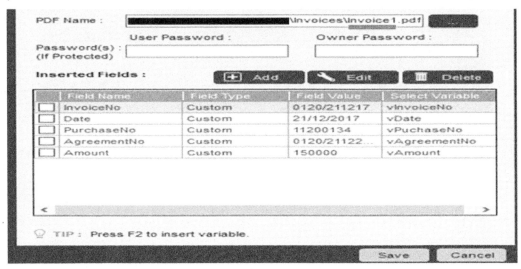

Figure 6.61: Original file path under PDF Name option

Click on the **Save** button as follows:

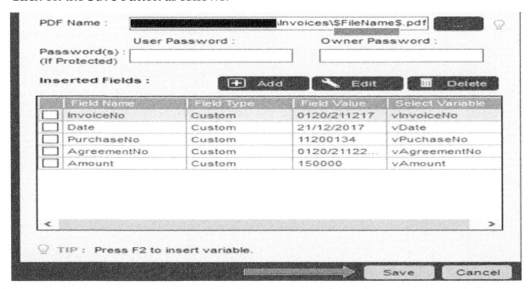

Figure 6.62: Modified file path with $FileName$ variable under PDF Name option

The next step is to use the **Excel** command and **Set Cell** and **Go To Cell** subcommands to write data in the Excel file cell by cell and move to the next row as done in the earlier tasks. The next step is to send an email with an Excel file as an attachment. Email settings have to be configured before the email can be sent and is a onetime process. Go to **Client Application**, and in **Tools** menu option, select the **Options** submenu option which will open the **Options** window as follows:

Figure 6.63: *Client Applications | Tools | Options*

Select the **Email Settings** option on the left in the **Options** window. Provide the email settings in the **Client Application** based on the settings of your email exchange server and click on the **Apply** button and then on the **OK** button as follows:

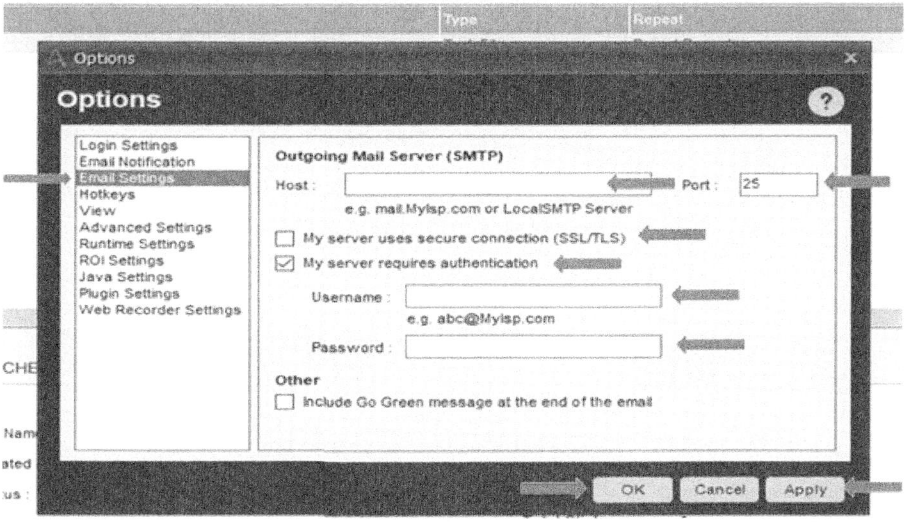

Figure 6.64: *Email settings under Options window*

Now, move back to **Workbench**. Use the **Excel** command and **Save Spreadsheet** and **Close Spreadsheet** subcommand just after the **End Loop** statement. Use the **Send Email** command and provide the values in the corresponding options, then click on the button with clip symbol to provide the path of the Excel file to be sent as an attachment, and click on the **Save** button as follows:

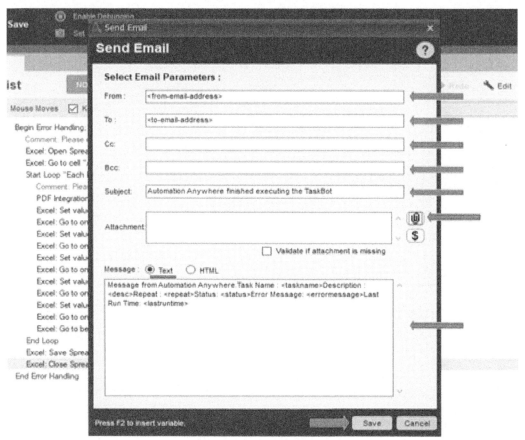

Figure 6.65: Send Email command

Next, implement the first step which is to download the invoices in the folder from the email. You should have an unread email with the invoices as an attachment as follows:

Figure 6.66: Sample email with invoices as attachment

Just after the **Begin Error Handling** statement, use the **Email Automation** command and **Get All Messages** subcommand and provide the IMAP or POP3 settings based on your email exchange server. Select the **Unread** option to iterate through only unread emails, the **Plain Text** option to download the email data in text format, under the **Save** attachments in options, provide the path of the folder given in the Loop command, and click on the **Save** button. The **Each Email Message On Mail Server** loop will be automatically generated as follows:

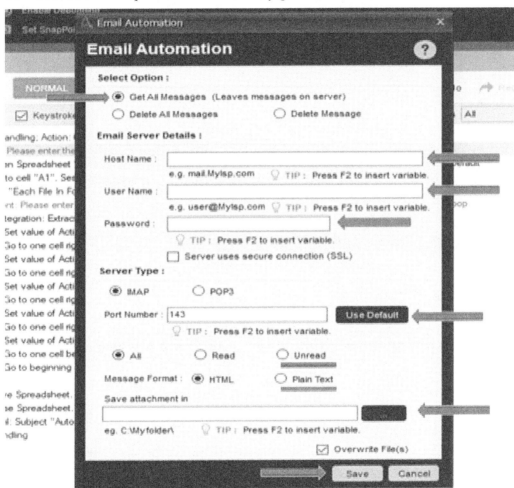

Figure 6.67: Email Automation command | Get All Messages subcommand

Inside the loop, use the **If Else** command and **Variable** sub command to filter the emails using the system variables for email as per your requirement. In this scenario, the emails will be filtered based on the subject line, and hence, the variable used for filtration will be EmailSubject. Click on the **Edit** button, in the **If Variable** window under **Variable** option, provide EmailSubject variable; using the Insert

Variable window, under **Operator** option, select **Includes** if you want a part of the subject line or **Equal To(=)** if you want exact subject line for identification, under the **Fix** option, provide the part of the exact subject line, and then, click on the **Save** button as follows:

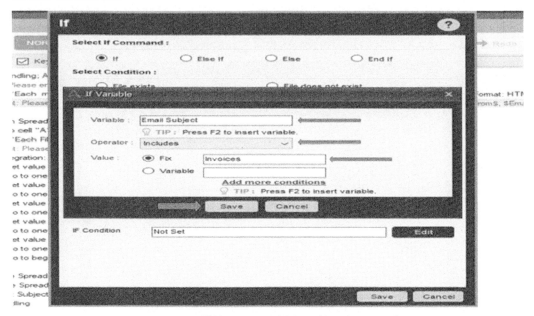

Figure 6.68: *If-Else command | Variable subcommand*

The complete task logic should now resemble the task logic provided as follows:

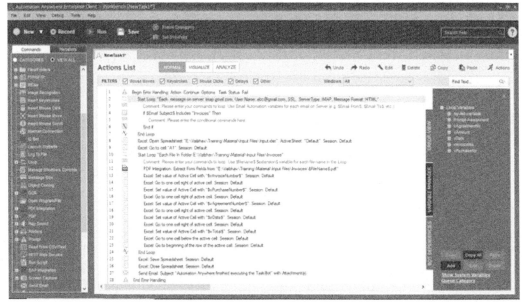

Figure 6.69: *Complete task logic*

Click on the **Save** button on the top and provide a meaningful task name, and then, click on the **Run** button to execute the bot and check the result in the Excel file and email.

> If you are using Gmail as an email server for sending and receiving emails, then open My Account page, click on the Security option on the left side, scroll down to the Less Secure Apps tab, and Turn on Access using the toggle button.

Conclusion

In this chapter, we discussed five use cases. The first use case was the Excel data extractor in which the data was extracted from the Excel sheet, propagated to a web application form, and then submitted to the database. The second use case was the web data extractor in which the data was extracted from a website table and saved in an Excel sheet. The third use case was the stock price infuser in which the share price of each company code was saved in the Excel sheet. The fourth use case was the database data extractor in which the data was extracted from the database and then saved in a CSV file. The last use case was the invoice processing in which invoices were downloaded from the email server, then the data extracted from invoices was saved into the Excel file, and the Excel file was sent as an attachment in the email. You can now work with multiple commands like Excel, database, object cloning, PDF, email, and more, and use them to automate the industry-standard use cases.

In the next chapter, we will discuss the commands left in the command library like XML, Web Services, PGP, OCR, and more.

Multiple choice questions

1. **Which variable is used in the Each Row In An Excel Dataset loop?**

    a. Dataset Column

    b. Excel Column

    c. Table Column

    d. Filedata Column

2. **Which variable is used in the Each Row In An Internet Explorer Table loop?**

    a. Table Column

    b. Dataset Column

    c. Excel Column

    d. None of the above

3. **Which variable is used in the Each Row In SQL Query Dataset loop?**

   a. Table Column

   b. Dataset Column

   c. Filedata Column

   d. None of the above

Answer

1. *b*
2. *a*
3. *b*

CHAPTER 7
Command Library

Introduction

In the last two chapters, we learned to work with many commands like Excel, database, CSV, PDF, and more. In this chapter, the rest of the commands in the command library will be discussed. These commands will help to create a bot logic as per the process flow, and the commands can be used in the bot logic as and when required. This chapter will discuss commands like String Operations, Web Services, XML, PGP, FTP, and more. In this chapter, each command will be discussed individually, and after learning the commands, you can use them together as per the requirement of your bot logic like done in the previous chapter.

Structure

In this chapter, we will discuss the following topics:

- Remaining commands in the command library like Web Services, XML, and String Operation, and more.

Objectives

After completing this chapter, you should be able to:

- Understand how to use the commands in the command library

Commands

In the last two chapters, we learned the usage of many commands like Excel, PDF, Database, CSV, Loop, and If Else. In this chapter, we will focus on the commands that are left in the command library and will be explored individually. You can use the commands discussed in this chapter as per the requirement of your process. The commands that are straight forward to use will be discussed as an overview.

Active Directory command

Active Directory is a central repository to register the human and physical resources in an organization. This command is used to automate the functionalities of Active Directory as follows:

Figure 7.1: Active Directory command

You need to provide the connection properties under the **Enter LDAP Path** option along with the login credentials, and then, you can use the subcommands like **Create User, Modify User, Create Group, Modify Group, Create Object, Modify Object, Search**, and **Get Property** to perform the related operations as follows:

- **App Integration command** is an obsolete command and the upgraded command for the same is OCR, which will be discussed later in the chapter.

- **Citrix Automation command** is an obsolete command and the upgraded functionality for the same is Citrix AISense under Metabot, which will be discussed later in *Chapter 8, Metabot.*

Clipboard command

The Clipboard command provides the functionality of copy and paste data into the clipboard and is very similar to the functionality of keyboard shortcut of *Ctrl + c* and *Ctrl + v*. The **Copy To Clipboard** subcommand is similar to *Ctrl + c*, and the **Copy From Clipboard** subcommand is similar to *Ctrl + v*.

- **Comment command** is used to insert the non-executable statements inside the task logic.

- **Database command** has already been discussed in the previous chapter.

Delay command

The Delay command is a combination of two commands which are Delay and Wait. Delay is used to provide a time interval between the executions of two commands in the task logic. Delay could be the **Regular Delay** option and mentioned in either milliseconds or seconds or mentioned as the **Random Delay** option. Let us say you have copied all the data from a PDF file using the keyboard shortcut *Ctrl + a* and *Ctrl + c* in the first command, and then, you want to paste the data into a Microsoft Word document using the *Ctrl + v* shortcut in the next command, then these two commands one after the other will fail. You will need to put a delay between the executions of the two commands for the automation to work as follows:

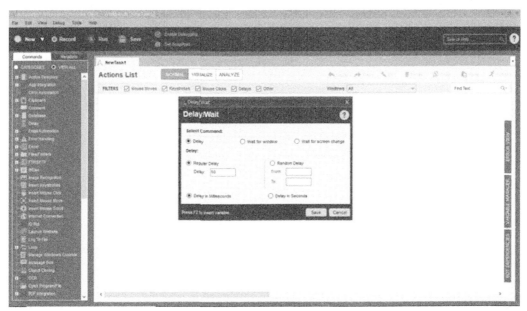

Figure 7.2: Delay command | Delay subcommand

The **Wait For Window** subcommand is used when you want to execute the next command based on the opening or the closing of a particular window as follows:

Figure 7.3: *Delay command | Wait For Window subcommand*

The **Wait For Screen Change** subcommand is used when the content is changing on the same screen without the change in the window title. This is a coordinate-based command and is not a very reliable command and should be used if no other command option can be employed as follows:

Figure 7.4: *Delay command | Wait For Screen Change subcommand*

- The Email Automation **command** has already been discussed in the previous chapter.

Error Handling command

Let us start with the task creation. Open **Workbench**. Click on the **New** button at the top of the **Workbench** window to create a new task bot. The next command to be discussed is **Error Handling**. The purpose of the **Error Handling** command is that when any runtime error occurs, the command logs the error and does not allow the system to be frozen and waits for a human intervention to move ahead to the next process. First, we will see what happens when a runtime error happens without the **Error Handling** command. To generate a runtime error, we will try to open a file that does not exist in the machine. Use the **Open Program/File** command, and in the **Program/File Path** option, provide the path of a non-existent file using the **Browse** button and then, click on the **Save** button as follows:

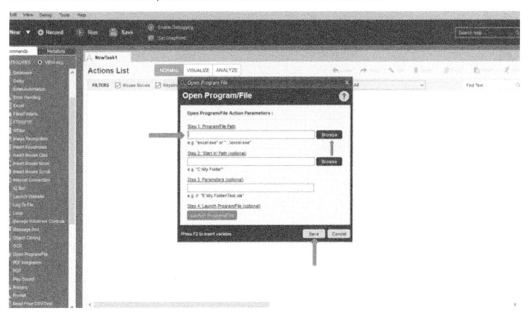

Figure 7.5: Open Program/File command without Error Handling command

Click on the **Save** button on the top and provide a meaningful task name, and then, click on the **Run** button to execute the bot and check the execution of the task logic.

It will generate an error message and the system will be frozen and the wait for a human intervention will continue as follows:

Figure 7.6: Runtime error without Error Handling command

Use the **Error Handling** command and bring the **Open Program/File** command inside the **Error Handling** block. Click on the **Save** button on the top, and then, click on the **Run** button to execute the bot and check the execution of the task logic. This time the runtime error will be managed by the **Error Handling** command and will not freeze the screen.

Let us now see the options available in the **Error Handling** command to log the error information during the execution. Double click on **Begin Error Handling** to see the available options. The first option to be explored is **Log Data Into File**. Select the **Log Data Into File** option and in the **Log File** option, provide the path of the text or CSV file in which you want to save the error information. Under the **Text** option, you can provide any information you want. If you want to save the date and time, line number and description of the error, then use the system variables, namely, **Date, Error Line Number**, and **Error Description** for the same as follows:

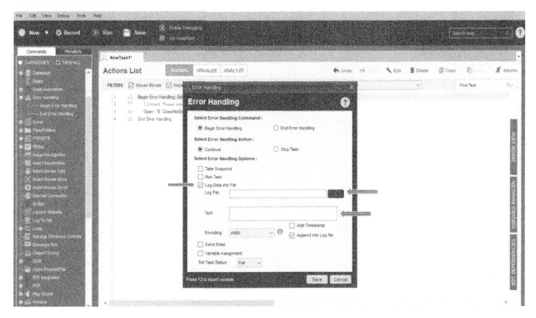

Figure 7.7: *Error Handling command | Log Data Into File option*

Use the **Take Snapshot** option to save the image of the error at the runtime. Under the **File Path** option, provide the path where the images are to be saved and give the name of the image file to be generated. Let us assume that the path for error screenshot is E:\Error Images\1.png. To make the path dynamic so that each image has a unique name, delete only 1 and press *F2* to open the **Insert Variable** window. Use the system variables, namely, Day, Month, Year, Hour, Minute, and Second to make the file name dynamic. The path will look like E:\Error Images\$Day$_$Month$_$Year$_$Hour$_$Minute$_$Second$.png. Based on your requirement, you can also use the Millisecond system variable as well. Using this technique, you can provide unique names to any type of file in any command as follows:

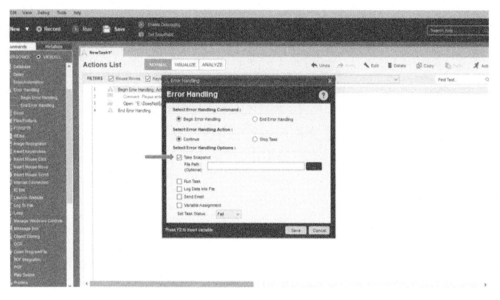

Figure 7.8: *Error Handling command | Take Snapshot option*

Use the **Run Task** option if you want any other task to be executed when an error is encountered. This option comes in handy when any other logic is to be executed when a runtime error is encountered. Under the **Select Task** option, provide the path of the pre-created task to be executed as follows:

Figure 7.9: *Error Handling command | Run Task option*

Let us say you want to send the error information as an attachment in the email; then, first you need to use the **Variable Assignment** option. Under the **Assign Variable** option on the left side under the **Specify Variable** option, press F2 and select the Prompt-Assignment variable, and on the right side under the Specify Value option, select the **Error Description** variable through the **Insert** variable window. Now, under the **Send Email** option, provide the **To, From**, and **Subject** options and select the **Attach Variable** option to send the error description as an attachment in the email. You can also attach the screenshot generated by the **Take Snapshot** option to be sent in the email using the **Attach Snapshot** option. Check the selected options and click on the **Save** button as follows:

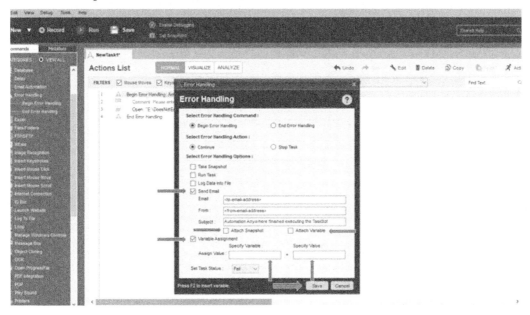

Figure 7.10: Error Handling command | Variable Assignment and Send Email option

> **The email will be sent only if the Email Settings are configured in the client application.**

Click on the **Save** button on the top, and then, click on the **Run** button to execute the bot and check the execution of the task logic.

The **Excel Command** has already been discussed in the previous chapter.

Files/Folders command

This command is used to create, rename, open, or delete files and folders. The subcommands available under the **File** options are **Create File, Copy Files, Rename Files, Delete Files, Zip Files, Unzip Files, Print File,**

Print Multiple Files, Open File, and **Create File Shortcut**. If you are trying to create a new Microsoft Office file like Word, Excel, or PowerPoint file using the **Create File** subcommand, then it will create a corrupted file, as Microsoft Office does not allow any third-party application to create the file. The Print File subcommand does not provide any **Print Preview** window at the runtime. Let us say you are printing a Word document, then whatever is the print setting in the Word document, those settings will be used by the **Print File** subcommand to perform the action as follows:

Figure 7.11: Files/ Folders command | subcommands under File option

The subcommands available under the **Folder** option are **Create Folder, Copy Folder, Rename Folder, Delete Folder, Open Folder**, and **Create Folder Shortcut** as follows:

Figure 7.12: Files/ Folders command | subcommands under Folder option

Using the Folder subcommands, you can create, copy, rename, delete, open, or create a folder shortcut provided you have the requisite privileges.

FTP/SFTP command

Click on the **New** button at the top of the **Workbench** window to create a new task bot. The next command to be discussed is **FTP/SFTP**. This command is used to connect to the FTP server and perform the various activities related to it provided you have the requisite permission from the administrator. Use the **FTP/SFTP** command and **Connect** subcommand to connect to your FTP server. Under the **FTP Server** option, provide the name of your FTP server. Under the **Username, Password** and **Port** option, provide the details given to you by the FTP server administrator. Under the **Secure Private Key File** option, provide the path of the secure key file if the server is secure FTP server by selecting the **Secure FTP** option on the right, and then, click the **on Test Connection** button to check that the connection to the FTP server has been established, and then, click on the **Save** button as follows:

Figure 7.13: FTP/SFTP command | Connect subcommand

Use the **FTP/SFTP** command and **Put Files** subcommand to upload the files to your FTP server provided you have the permission for the same. Under the **Local Files** option, provide the path of the file(s) to be uploaded, and then, click on the **Save** button as follows:

Figure 7.14: FTP/SFTP command | Put Files subcommand

Use the **FTP/SFTP** command and **Disconnect** subcommand to disconnect from the FTP server. Click on the **Save** button on the top and provide a meaningful task name, and then, click on the **Run** button to execute the bot and check the execution of the task logic. All the other subcommands under the **FTP/SFTP** command can be implemented similarly.

The **If/Else** command is used to execute the task logic based on the conditions and its implementation using the **Variable** subcommand, which has already been discussed in the previous chapter. The other subcommands for creating the condition-based task logic execution available are **File Exists or not**, **Folder Exists or not**, **Window Exists or not**, **Application (.exe) Running or not**, **Script (VBScript or JavaScript) Successful or not**, **Task Successful or Not**, **Ping Successful or not**, **Variable**, **Web Control**, **File Date**, **File Size**, **Service (Background Windows Services) Running or not**, **Image Recognition**, **Windows Control and Object Properties**. **Web Control**, and

Windows Control are obsolete commands and instead **Object Properties** should be used that uses the **Object Cloning** command as follows:

Figure 7.15: *If/Else command*

The **Image Recognition** command is an obsolete command and was used for a button click in the Citrix environment. The upgraded functionality for the same is Citrix AISense under Metabot, which will be discussed later in *Chapter 8, Metabot*.

Insert Keystrokes command

Click on the **New** button at the top of the **Workbench** window to create a new task bot. The next command to be discussed is **Insert Keystrokes**. It is one of the most reliable commands in Automation Anywhere, as the keyboard shortcuts work the same across the different systems. This command is used to implement keyboard shortcuts during the execution of the task logic. Create a text file with the name `Attendance.txt` and use F5 to register the timestamps in the text file and then save the file. Open the **Run** window separately as well. The first step in the automation will be to take the **Begin Error Handling** subcommand under the **Error Handling** command in the **Workbench**. Use the **Insert keystrokes** command, and under the **Select Window** option, select the **Currently Active Window** option. Under the **Keystrokes** option, provide **[WinDown]r[WinUp]** by clicking the **WinDown** key in the virtual keyboard and then, write r directly from the keyboard and then click on the **WinDown** key in the virtual keyboard, as it mimics the pressing of the **Win** key with r in combination and then release the Win key. Under the **Delay** option, insert 500, as this option is in milliseconds, and then, click on the **Save** button as follows:

Figure 7.16: *Insert Keystrokes command to open Run window*

Use the **Insert keystrokes** command and under the **Select Window** option select the **Run** option. Under the **Keystrokes** option provide the full path of the **Attendance.txt** file, and then, click **Enter key** from the virtual keyboard. Under **Delay** option, insert 500, as this option is in milliseconds, and then, click on the **Save** button as follows:

Figure 7.17: *Insert Keystrokes command to open Attendance.txt file*

Use the **Insert keystrokes** command and under the **Select Window** option, select **Attendance-Notepad** option. Under the **Keystrokes** option provide *[CtrlDown] [End][CtrlUp][Enter][F5][CtrlUp]s[CtrlDown][AltUp][F4][AltDown]* from the virtual keyboard. *[CtrlDown][End][CtrlUp][Enter]* is used to reach to a new line in the text file to append the content. *[F5][CtrlUp]s[CtrlDown]* is used to register the timestamp and then, save the content, and *[AltUp][F4][AltDown]* is used to close the text file. Under the **Delay** option, insert 500, as this option is in milliseconds, and then, click on the **Save** button. Click on the **Save** button on the top and provide a meaningful task name, and then, click on the **Run** button to execute the bot and check the execution of the task logic as follows:

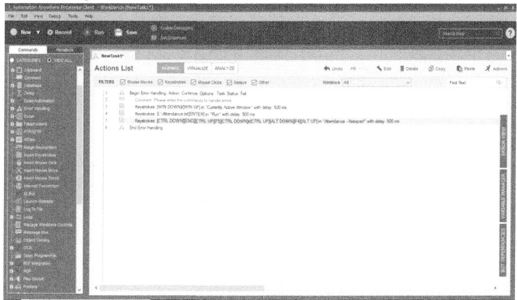

Figure 7.18: *Complete task logic*

- The Insert Mouse Click, Insert Mouse Move, and Insert Mouse Scroll **commands** are used to mimic the mouse actions, and the usage is not preferred, as they are coordinate-based commands and are not reliable commands.

- The Internet Connection **command** is an obsolete command and is used to test the connectivity to the DSL internet connection.

- The IQ Bot **command** will be discussed later in *Chapter 11, IQ Bot*.

- The Launch Website **command** is used to open the website in the system default browser.

- The Log To File and Loop **command** has already been discussed in the previous chapter.

- The Manage Windows Control **command** is an obsolete command and the upgraded command is the **Object Cloning** command, which has already been discussed.

- The Message Box and Object Cloning **command** have already been discussed in the previous chapter.

OCR command

OCR stands for **Optical Character Recognition,** and this command is used to read text from image files. The first step will be to take the **Begin Error Handling** subcommand under the **Error Handling** command. Use the **OCR** command and **Capture Area** subcommand, and under the **Select Window** option, provide the window in which you want to capture the area from which the data will be captured. The OCR engines provided are **ABBY**, **MODI**, **TESSERACT**, and **TOCR**. **TESSERACT** can be used out of the box, but the other engines require a license to be used. Click on the **Capture Area** button to select the area from which the text will be extracted. Click on the **View Captured Text** button to preview the extracted text. Under the **Assign the value to an existing variable** option, select the **Prompt-Assignment** variable and click on the **Save** button as follows:

Figure 7.19: OCR command | Capture Area subcommand

Use the **Message Box** command and provide the **Prompt-Assignment** variable as the message and click on the **Save** button. Click on the **Save** button on the top and provide a meaningful task name, and then, click on the **Run** button to execute the bot and check the execution of the task. The **Capture Window** subcommand will extract the text from the specified window. The **Capture Image By Path** subcommand will extract the text from an image saved on the system. The **Capture Image By URL** subcommand will extract the text from an image on the internet location.

Open Program/File command

This command is used to open files or applications (`.exe`). It can also be used to open Command Prompt or Power Shell. Under the **Program File/Path** option provide the full path of the file or application you want to open. Under the **Start In Path** option, you can provide the startup path of the folder. Under the **Parameters** option, you can provide the parameters for the file or application you want to open. The command-line arguments can be provided under the **Parameters** option for your application if required as follows:

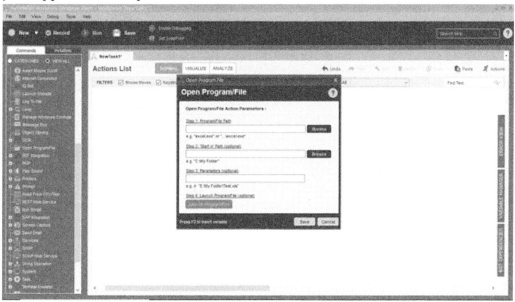

Figure 7.20: *Open Program/File command*

The PDF Integration **command** has already been discussed in the previous chapter.

PGP command

The PGP command is used to encrypt and decrypt the content inside the file. There are two following modes of encryption in the PGP command:

- **Passphrase:** The same phrase is used to encrypt and decrypt files. It is very similar to the lock in your house in which the same key is used to lock and unlock.

- **Public/Private Key:** The Public key is used for encryption and is a combination of the public and the private key is used for decryption. It is very similar to your bank account locker, where to open your locker, you need your key as well as the master key from the banker.

Click on the **New** button at the top of the **Workbench** window to create a new task bot. The sample text for encryption is as follows:

Encrypt - Notepad

File   Edit   Format   View   Help

This is an encrypted file.

Figure 7.21: Sample plain text in the file

The first step will be to take the **Begin Error Handling** subcommand under the **Error Handling** command. Use the **Encrypt Files** subcommand under the **PGP** command, and under the **Passphrase** option, provide the phrase that you want to be used as the key for encryption. Under the **Symmetric Algorithm** option, select the algorithm that you want to be used for encrypting the text. Under the **Source File(s)/ Folder** option, provide the path of the file or files under the folder to be encrypted, and under the **Destination File(s)/ Folder** option, provide the full path of the folder in which the file will be saved along with a new file name such as **Encrypted.txt**. Select the **Overwrite Files/ Folders** option. If the **Armor Data** option is left unselected, then the encrypted text will be in the non-readable format, and if it is selected, then a readable gibberish text will be generated. Click on the **Save** button as follows:

Figure 7.22: PGP command | Encrypt File subcommand

Click on the **Save** button on the top and provide a meaningful task name, and then, click on the **Run** button to execute the bot and check that a new file with the encrypted text has been generated.

Use the **Decrypt Files** subcommand under the **PGP** command, and under the **Passphrase** option, provide the same phrase that you provided as the key to beused for encryption. Under the **Source File(s)/ Folder** option, provide the path of the **Encrypted.txt** file, and under the **Destination File(s)/ Folder** option, provide the full path of the folder in which the file will be saved along with a new file **Decrypted.txt**. Select the **Overwrite Files/ Folders** option and click on the **Save** button as follows:

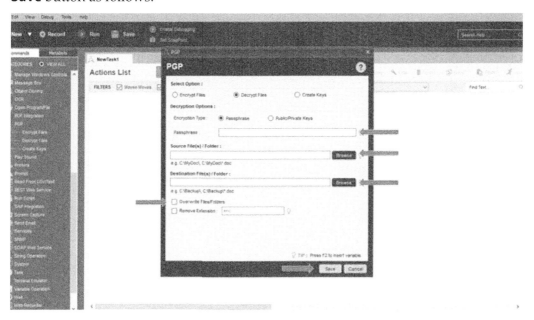

Figure 7.23: PGP command | Decrypt File subcommand

Click on the **Save** button on the top, and then, click on the **Run** button to execute the bot and check that a new file with plain text has been generated.

Click on the **New** button at the top of the **Workbench** window to create a new task bot. The first step will be to take the **Begin Error Handling** subcommand under the **Error Handling** command. Use the **Create Keys** subcommand under the **PGP** command. Under the **Public Key File** option provide the filename with .pkr extension along with the full path of the file. Under the **Private Key File** option, provide the filename with .pkr extension along with the full path of the file. You can provide a password to pass along with the keys for encryption and decryption as an extra protection measure under the **Password** option and click on the **Save** button as follows:

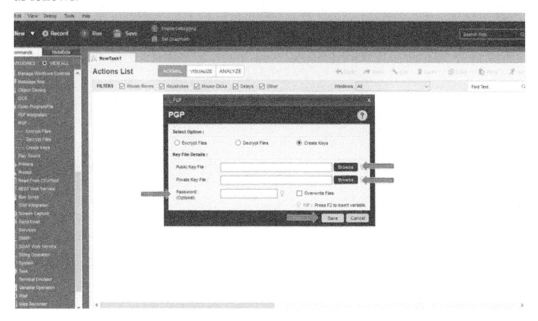

Figure 7.24: *PGP command | Create Keys subcommand*

Click on the **Save** button on the top and provide a meaningful task name, and then, click on the **Run** button to execute the bot and check that the public and private key files have been generated. Repeat the same process for encrypting and decrypting the file as in the previous task, and instead of passphrase, provide the public key for encryption and the private key for decryption.

- The Play Sound **command** is used to play a beep sound using the **Play Beep** subcommand or play an audio file using the **Play Media File** subcommand.

- The Printer **command** is used to get and set the default printer using **Get Default Printer** and **Set Default Printer** subcommand or remove a printer from the network using the **Remove Printer** subcommand.

- The Prompt **command** has already been discussed in the previous chapter.

Read From CSV/Text command

Click on the **New** button at the top of the **Workbench** window to create a new task bot. This command is used to read data from either the CSV or text files. The sample data in the CSV file is as follows:

Id	Name	Age
101	ABC	20
102	ABD	22
103	ABE	24
104	ABF	20

Table 7.1: *Sample data in CSV file*

The first step will be to take the **Begin Error Handling** subcommand under the **Error Handling** command. Use the **Read From CSV/Text** command, and under the **Select File** option, provide the full path of the CSV file. Select the **Delimiter** option as a comma. Select the **Contains Header** option if the data in your CSV file has headings in the first column as the case in the sample data. Select the **Leading Spaces and Trailing Spaces** option to trim the text and click on the **Save** button as follows:

Figure 7.25: *Read From CSV/ Text command*

Each Row in a **CSV/Text File** loop will be automatically generated and the variable to access the column values will be **FileData Column**. Inside the loop, use the **Message Box** command and provide FileData Column(1), FileData Column(2), FileData Column(3) as a message using *F2* and **Insert Variable** window, and click on the **Save** button. Click on the **Save** button on the top and provide a meaningful task name, and then, click on the **Run** button to execute the bot and check the execution of the task logic. Repeat the same process for reading the data from the text file.

REST Web Service command

Click on the **New** button at the top of the **Workbench** window to create a new task bot. The next command to be discussed is the REST web service. This command is used to call the REST web service in your process. Let us use a free online available REST web service with the URI **https://reqres.in/api/users?page=2**. The first step will be to take the **Begin Error Handling** subcommand under the **Error Handling** command. Use the REST Web Service command and under the URI option provide **https://reqres.in/api/users?page=2**. Based on the requirement and documentation of your web service select either GET, POST, PUT, or DELETE under the **Method** option and authentication details under the **Parameter** tab and click on the **Send Request** button. In this scenario, directly click on the **Send Request** button and click on the **Response** tab as follows:

Figure 7.26: REST Web Service command | Request tab

Under the **Response** tab and **Header** option, you can see the **Content-Type** as application/json in the table that implies that the returned data is in JSON format. Click on the **Body** option on the left side if you want to see the response from the web service. You can save the header data and response data in the variables you want.

Let us save the response data in the **Prompt-Assignment** variable and click on the **Save** button as follows:

Figure 7.27: REST Web Service command | Response tab

Use the **Message Box** command and provide the **Prompt-Assignment** variable as the message. Click on the **Save** button on the top and provide a meaningful task name, and then, click on the **Run** button to execute the bot and check the execution of the task logic.

Run Script command

Click on the **New** button at the top of the **Workbench** window to create a new task bot. The next command to be discussed is the Run Script. This command is used to execute either the VBScript or JavaScript code stored in the file in your process. The sample JavaScript code is as follows:

```
WScript.StdOut.WriteLine(Date());
```

The first step will be to take the **Begin Error Handling** subcommand under the **Error Handling** command. Use the **Run Script** command and under the **Select Script** option, provide the path of the JavaScript file using the **Browse** button. If your JavaScript code requires any input parameters, provide them under the **Parameters** option each separated by a comma. In this scenario leave it blank, and in the **Return**

Value option, provide the **Prompt-Assignment** variable using *F2* and click on the **Save** button as follows:

Figure 7.28: *Run Script command*

Use the **Message Box** command and provide the **Prompt-Assignment** variable as a message. Click on the **Save** button on the top and provide a meaningful task name, and then, click on the **Run** button to execute the bot and check the execution of the task logic. Change the path of the file to the **VBScript** file to execute the VBScript code and provide the **Parameters** and **Return Value** option accordingly.

The SAP Integration **command** is an obsolete command and the upgraded functionality for the same is Citrix AISense under Metabot, which will be discussed later in *Chapter 8, Metabot*.

Screen Capture command

This command is used to capture the screenshot of the desktop, selected window, or area and save it at the given location. Click on the **New** button at the top of the **Workbench** window to create a new task bot. The first step will be to take the **Begin Error Handling** subcommand under the **Error Handling** command. Use the **Capture Desktop** subcommand under the **Screen Capture** command, and under the **Specify Image Location** option, provide the file name of the image along with the full path and click on the **Save** button as follows:

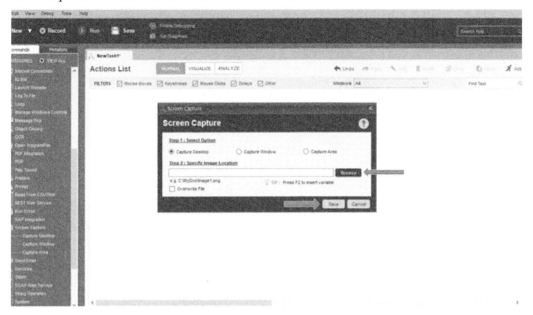

Figure 7.29: *Screen Capture command | Capture Desktop subcommand*

Click on the **Save** button on the top and provide a meaningful task name and then click on the **Run** button to execute the bot and check the execution of the task logic. Repeat the same process for capturing the screenshot of a particular window or an area.

The Send Email **command** has already been discussed in the previous chapter.

Services command

This command is used to start, stop, pause, resume, or check the status of a particular windows service. You will need the access privileges to perform the actions on windows services. Click on the **New** button at the top of the **Workbench** window to create a new task bot. The first step will be to take the **Begin Error Handling** subcommand under the **Error Handling** command. Use the **Get Service Status** subcommand under the **Services** command and select the service whose status you want to check under the **Available installed services on this machine** option, and under the **Assign** the value to an existing variable option, select the **Prompt-Assignment** variable and click on the **Save** button as follows:

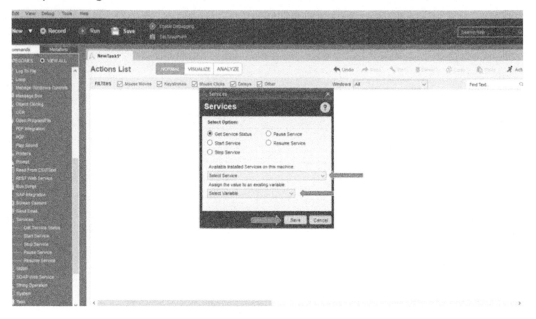

Figure 7.30: *Services command | Get Service Status subcommand*

Use the **Message Box** command and provide the **Prompt-Assignment** variable as the message. Click on the **Save** button on the top and provide a meaningful task name, and then, click on the **Run** button to execute the bot and check the execution of the task logic. Repeat the same process to start, stop, pause, or resume a service provided you have the required privileges.

SNMP command

SNMP stands for Simple Network Management Protocol, and it is an application-layer protocol used to manage and monitor network devices and their functions and is mainly used to automate the task of the networking team. Click on the **New** button at the top of the **Workbench** window to create a new task bot. The first step will be to take the **Begin Error Handling** subcommand under the **Error Handling** command. Use the **Get** subcommand under the **SNMP** command and provide the address of the agent program under the **Agent** option. Under the **Object ID** option, provide the address of the device, and under the **Assign the value to**

an existing variable, select **Prompt-Assignment** variable and click on the **Save** button as follows:

Figure 7.31: *SNMP command | Get subcommand*

Use the **Message Box** command and provide the **Prompt-Assignment** variable as a message. Click on the **Save** button on the top and provide a meaningful task name, and then, click on the **Run** button to execute the bot and check the execution of the task logic. Repeat the same process for **Get Next**, **Set**, **Walk**, and **Send Trap** subcommands.

SOAP Web Service command

Click on the **New** button at the top of the Workbench window to create a new task bot. The next command to be discussed is the SOAP web service. This command is used to call the SOAP web service in your process. Let us use a free online available SOAP web service with the URI **http://www.dneonline.com/calculator.asmx**. The first step will be to take the **Begin Error Handling** subcommand under the **Error Handling** command. Use the **SOAP Web Service** command, and under the **Enter**

Complete URI, option click on the **Build** button to open the **Build SOAP Web Service URI** window as follows:

Figure 7.32: SOAP Web Service command

Under the **Enter WSDL URI** option provide **http://www.dneonline.com/calculator. asmx?WSDL** and click on the **Connect** button. Select the service, port, version, and operation based on your requirement and the documentation provided by your web service vendor. In this particular web service, choose either of the four operations and provide the parameter values under Step 7 by clicking the parameter name like intA in the table and providing a static value or a variable under the **Value** option and then, click on the **Update** button. Repeat the same process for the second parameter intB and then, click on the **Save** button as follows:

Figure 7.33: SOAP Web Service command | Build SOAP Web Service URI window

If your web service requires authentication, then provide a username, password, domain name, and client certificate whichever is required under the **Authentication Details** option. In this scenario, leave it blank and click on the **Test Output** button. You can save the output in an XML file or transfer the whole or partial output to a variable. To extract a particular value or partial output, select the **Select/View Response** link under the **Selected Response** option. You can select the desired value by expanding the soap envelope nodes. Under the **Assign the returned value to an existing** variable option, select **Prompt-Assignment** variable and click on the **Save** button as follows:

Figure 7.34: *SOAP Web Service command*

Use the `Message Box` command and provide the **Prompt-Assignment** variable as `message`. Click on the **Save** button on the top and provide a meaningful task name, and then, click on the **Run** button to execute the bot and check the execution of the task logic.

String Operation command

Click on the **New** button at the top of the **Workbench** window to create a new task bot. The next command to be discussed is **String Operation**. This command is used to manipulate strings. The first step will be to take the **Begin Error Handling** subcommand under the **Error Handling** command. Use the **String Operation** command and **Before-After** subcommand and under the **Source String** option, provide the string text to be manipulated like Johny Johny Yes Papa Eating Sugar No Papa in this instance. Under the **Before** option, provide Johny as value and under the **After** option, provide Papa as value, and under the **Assign the**

value to an existing variable option, select the **Prompt-Assignment** variable and click on the **Save** button as follows:

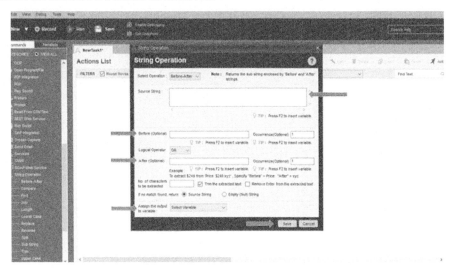

Figure 7.35: String Operation command | Before-After subcommand

Use the **Message Box** command and provide the **Prompt-Assignment** variable as message. Click on the **Save** button on the top and provide a meaningful task name, and then, click on the **Run** button to execute the bot. The output will be Johny Yes. If you want that the output should be Johny Yes Papa Eating Sugar No, or you want the text to be extracted between the first appearance of Johny and second appearance of Papa in the text, then provide 2 as the value under the **Occurrence** option next to the **After** option where Papa is provided as the value and click on the **Save** button as follows:

Figure 7.36: String Operation command | Before-After subcommand with 2 as value for Occurrence option

Click on the **Save** button on the top and then, click on the **Run** button to execute the bot and check the output. The other subcommands under the **String Operation** command are **Compare**, **Find**, **Join**, **Length**, **Lower Case**, **Replace**, **Reverse**, **Split**, **Sub String**, **Trim**, and **Upper Case** and are pretty straight forward to use.

System command

This command is used to lock, log off, shut down, or restart the system. The main functionality that is created using this command is that the task at the time of the execution will automatically login to the system, execute the task logically, and lock the system using the **System** command. Click on the **New** button at the top of the **Workbench** window to create a new task bot. The first step will be to take the **Begin Error Handling** subcommand under the **Error Handling** command. Use a **Message Box** command with **Hello** as the message and close the message box after 2 seconds. Again, use a **Message Box** command with **Hi** as the message and close the message box after 2 seconds. Use the **System** command and **Lock Computer** subcommand as follows:

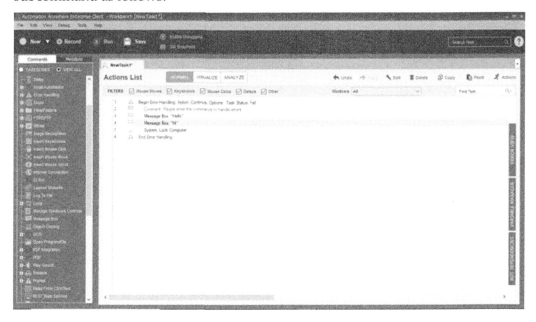

Figure 7.37: *Complete task logic*

Click on the **Save** button on the top and provide a meaningful task name. Now, at the runtime, the task will be executed and the system will be locked after the completion of the task logic. The next steps will be done, so at the runtime, the task can automatically login to the system. Go to the **Client Application** and select the just created task and click the **Schedule** tab and under the **Launch Task** option, select **One Time Only** as follows:

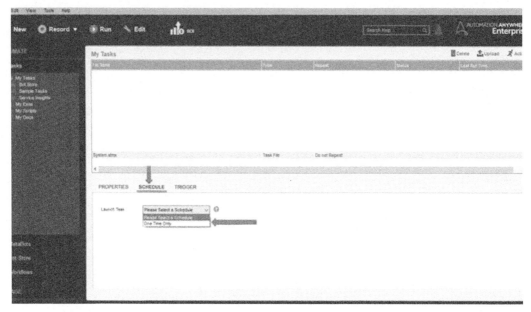

Figure 7.38: *Client Application | Schedule tab | One time only value*

Under the **Start Time** and **Start Date** option, provide the date and time for automatic execution of the bot and click on the **Save** button that will open the **Credential for Creating Schedule** window as follows:

Figure 7.39: *Client Application | Schedule tab | One time only value | Start Time and Start Date option*

In the **Credential for Creating Schedule** window, provide the credentials used to login to the machine under the **Username** and **Password** option. Select the **Always use the above credential to schedule and run task(s)** and **Enable Auto Login** options and click on the **Save** button as follows:

Figure 7.40: *Client Application | Schedule tab | One time only value |*
Credentials for Creating Schedule window

Now, lock the system, and the task will automatically login to the system at the specified date and time; execute the task, and then, lock the system again.

Task command

This command is used to create a workflow by executing one task after the other. Two tasks will be created, and the first task will be called and executed in the second task along with the transfer of values of variables from the first task to variables of the second task. Click on the **New** button at the top of the **Workbench** window to create a new task bot. The first step will be to take the **Begin Error Handling** subcommand under the **Error Handling** command, and then, create two variables of value type named vNum1T1 and vNum2T1 with a null value and use the **Prompt**

For Value subcommand under the **Prompt** command to take the input from the user in the variables as follows:

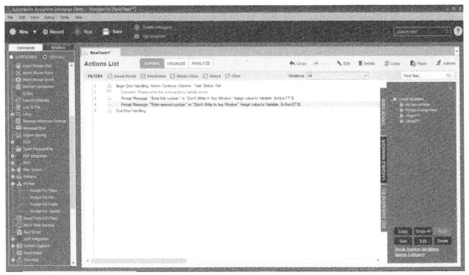

Figure 7.41: Complete task logic of Task1

Click on the **Save** button on the top and provide Task1 as the name of the task. Click on the **New** button at the top of the **Workbench** window to create a new task bot. The first step will be to take the **Begin Error Handling** subcommand under the **Error Handling** command, and then, create three variables of the value type named vNum1T2, vNum2T1, and vResult with the null value. Use the **Task** command and select the **Run Task** subcommand and under the **Select Task** option, select Task1 and then, select **Variable** option as follows:

Figure 7.42: Task command | Run Task subcommand

Under the **Main Task Variable** option, select vNum1T2, and under the **Run Task Variable** option, select vNum1T1 and click on the **Add** button and repeat the same process for mapping of the variables vNum2T2 and vNum2T1 and click on the **Save** button as follows:

Figure 7.43: *Task command | Run Task sub command | Variable mapping*

Use the **Variable Operation** command with the selection from the dropdown list being vResult on the left side and expression being vNum1T2+vNum2T2 on the right side. Use the **Message Box** command and provide the vResult variable as the message. Click on the **Save** button on the top and provide a meaningful task name and then, click on the **Run** button to execute the bot and check the execution of the task logic.

Terminal Emulator command

Click on the **New** button at the top of the **Workbench** window to create a new task bot. The next command to be discussed is Terminal Emulator. This command is used to work with legacy systems like Mainframe, Delphi, and more, and perform various activities related to it provided you have the requisite permission from the administrator. Use the **Terminal Emulator** command and **Connect** subcommand to connect to your legacy mainframe system and provide the values as per your mainframe machine under the **Terminal Type**, **Terminal Model**, **Host Name**, **Port**,

Connection Type, and **Terminal Prompt** message to appear on the mainframe window and then, click on the **Save** button as follows:

Figure 7.44: *Terminal Emulator command | Connect subcommand*

Use the **Terminal Emulator** command and the **Send Text** subcommand to send a text to your mainframe system provided you have the permission for the same. Under the **Text** option, provide the text you want to send to the mainframe system. Under the **Send a key after sending the above text** option, select the key you want to send like Enter, and under the **Wait for Terminal Prompt to appear** option, select **After** sending the text and then, click on the **Save** button as follows:

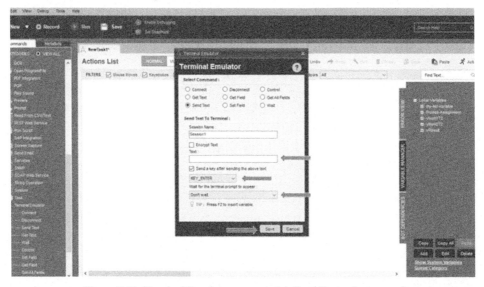

Figure 7.45: *Terminal Emulator command | Send Text subcommand*

Use the **Terminal Emulator** command and the **Disconnect** subcommand to disconnect from the mainframe system. Click on the **Save** button on the top and provide a meaningful task name, and then, click on the **Run** button to execute the bot and check the execution of the task logic. All the other subcommands under **Terminal Emulator** command can be implemented similarly.

- The Variable Operation command has already been discussed in the previous chapter.
- The Wait command has already been discussed earlier in the chapter along with the Delay command.
- The web recorder and Window Actions command has already been discussed in the previous chapter.

XML command

Click on the **New** button at the top of the **Workbench** window to create a new task bot. The next command to be discussed is XML. This command is used to manipulate the XML data. The sample XML data is as follows:

```
<?xml version="1.0" encoding="UTF-8"?>

<note>
  <to>Tove</to>
  <from>Jani</from>
  <heading>Reminder</heading>
  <body>Don't Forget The Meeting On The Weekend!</body>
</note>
```

The first step will be to take the **Begin Error Handling** subcommand under the **Error Handling** command. Use the **XML** command and **Start XML Session** subcommand and under the **Data Source** option, provide either the path of the XML file or the XML text and click on the **Save** button as follows:

Figure 7.46: XML command | Start XML Session subcommand

Let us say you want to add a new element in the XML data, and the position of the new element should be the first child element or just after the note element which is the parent element. Use the **XML** command and **Insert Node** subcommand at Line 4. Under the **XPath Expression** option, provide //note, *as you want to access the note element* and // is the syntax for **XPath** in the XML. Under the **Node Name** option, provide the date and under the **Node Value** option, provide the current date manually. Under the **Insert node location** option, use the pre-selected option **Beginning of the child nodes as the new element** that should be the first child element and click on the **Save** button:

Figure 7.47: XML command | Insert New Node subcommand

Use the **XML** command and the **Get Node(s)** subcommand to extract the value of the element date that was inserted in the last command. Under the **XPath Expression** option, provide //date, as *the date is the element to be accessed*. Under **Assign value to variable** option, select the **Prompt-Assignment** variable from the dropdown list and click on the **Save** button as follows:

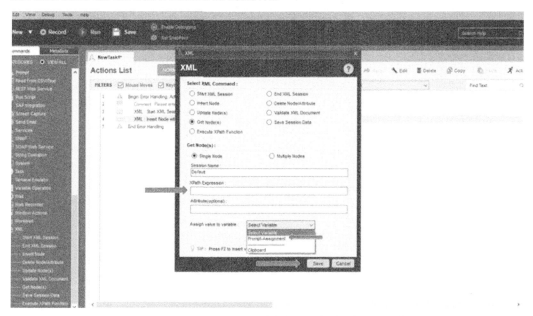

Figure 7.48: XML command | Get Node(s) subcommand

Use the **Message Box** command and provide the **Prompt-Assignment** variable as message and click on the **Save** button. Click on the **Save** button on the top and provide a meaningful task name, and then, click on the **Run** button to execute the bot and check the execution of the task logic till here. The value provided in the date element will be shown in the message box at the runtime, but the date element will not be reflected in the XML file. Use the **XML** command and the **Save Session Data** subcommand to reflect the date element in the XML file. Under the **Assign XML data to variable** option, select the **Clipboard** variable from the dropdown list. Select the **Write XML Data** option and under the **File Path** option, provide the path for a new XML file to be generated. You can also give the path of the original

XML file as well, but as a best practice, changes should be saved in a separate XML file. Select the **Overwrite File** option and click on the **Save** button as follows:

Figure 7.49: *XML command | Save Session Data subcommand*

Click on the **Save** button on the top, and then, click on the **Run** button to execute the bot and check that the new element will now be reflected in the XML file. Just succeeding the **Message Box** command, use the **XML** command and **Update Node(s)** subcommand to update the value of the date element. Under the **XPath Expression** option, provide //date, and under the **New Value** option, provide the **Date system** variable using *F2* and click on the **Save** button as follows:

Figure 7.50: *XML command | Update Node(s) subcommand*

Just before the **End Error Handling** statement, use the **XML** command and **End XML Session** subcommand as follows:

Figure 7.51: Complete task logic

Now, again click on the **Save** button on the top and then, click on the **Run** button to execute the bot again and check the updated value.

Conclusion

In this chapter, we discussed the commands that were left in the command library like Error Handling, Files/ Folders, FTP/SFTP, Insert Keystrokes, OCR, PGP, Read From CSV/Text, String Operation, System, Task, and XML. After completing this chapter, you can now use these commands to create a bot logic as per the requirement of your process flow and the commands can be used in the bot logic as and when required.

In the next chapter, we will discuss the Metabot, which is the new industry standard for creating task logic. The advantages provided by using Metabot are Offline development, DLL execution, and simpler capturing of objects in Standard and Remote Desktop, Virtual Machine (VM), Citrix, and SAP environment.

Multiple choice questions

1. **Which variable is used in the Each Row In An CSV/Text loop?**

    a. Dataset Column

    b. Excel Column

    c.   Table Column

    d.   Filedata Column

2. **Task command is used to create _____.**

    a.   Report

    b.   Metabot

    c.   Workflow

    d.   None of the above

3. **SNMP stands for _____.**

    a.   Simple Network Management Protocol

    b.   Source Network Management Protocol

    c.   Simple Network Manager Protocol

    d.   None of the above

Answers

   1. *d*

   2. *c*

   3. *a*

CHAPTER 8

Metabot

Introduction

In the previous chapters, you learned to create the task bots. In this chapter, a different approach to create automation logic will be discussed which is known as Metabots. The new industry standard for creating the bot logic is using a Metabot, as they provide many advantages over taskbots, with the prominent being Offline Development, Ability to execute DLL, and Citrix AISense. Citrix AISense is used to capture objects in Remote Desktop, **Virtual Machine** (**VM**), Citrix, and SAP environments.

Structure

In this chapter, we will discuss the following topics:

- Development of metabots
- Advantages of metabots
- Citrix AISense

Objectives

After completing this chapter, you should be able to:

- Understand how to develop metabots
- Understand how to use metabots to create automation for Citrix, Remote, and SAP environments

Metabot

In the previous chapters, automation logic was developed using Task bot, which has the extension `atmx`. In this chapter, we will focus on a different approach to develop automation logic by using metabot. The extension of metabot is `mbot`. The industry has progressed towards the creation of automation logic through metabot and is the preferred choice. The metabot does not execute standalone and has to be called inside a task bot (`atmx`) for the execution.

The advantages of using the metabot are as follows:

- **Offline Development (Screenshots)**: If you had to capture objects using the Object Cloning command in task bot, then the application has to be open while capturing the objects. If you're using a metabot for the same purpose, then you can just capture the screenshot of the application and work on the automation or capturing of the objects at a later stage even if the application is not open.

- **Separation of UI & Logic**: There is a separate interface for screenshots and DLL and different interfaces to create logic using the command library.

- **Usage of DLL**: **Dynamic Link Library (DLL)** is a piece of code that does not have a UI and is very useful in certain scenarios where you need to execute the .NET code stored in the DLL. Using metabot, you can call and execute the DLL in Automation Anywhere.

- **Citrix AISense**: This new feature has been provided in Automation Anywhere v11. It is used to capture objects of applications running in Citrix, SAP, and Remote Desktop environments. It has eased automation in these environments considerably.

- **Reusability**: The metabot once created can be used in multiple task bots and, hence, provides reusability, very similar to the Run Task command.

You need to have the Metabot Designer role assigned to your user credentials to create a metabot. The role was assigned while creating the user credentials in *Chapter 4: Client Application*.

In the example to be discussed, the data will be captured from the excel file and uploaded to a form and then saved in the database exactly like in the Excel data processing use case in *Chapter 6: Use Cases*. Open the application form in which the data will be uploaded beforehand. Open the Client Application and click on the **MetaBots** option as follows:

Figure 8.1: Client Application | Metabots option

Click on the **New Metabot** button on the right-hand corner to open **New Metabot** window as follows:

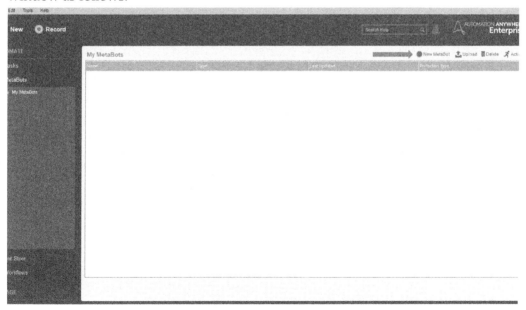

Figure 8.2: Metabots option | New Metabot option

In the **New Metabot** window, provide a name for the metabot under the **New Metabot** option, and under the **Metabot Type** option, select **Application Specific** and select **Internet Explorer,** as the application form whose controls have to be captured is opened in the internet explorer and click on the **Create** button to open the **Metabot Designer** window as follows:

Figure 8.3: New Metabot window | Internet Explorer application

If you have opened the form in any other browser, select that browser. If your use case is such that you have to capture the data from an online form and save the data in an ERP application, then select **All Application** option under the **Metabot Type** option as you will need to capture the screenshots from multiple applications.

In the **Metabot Designer** window, under the **Assets** tab, click on the **Add Screen** button to capture the application form whose objects are to be captured and open the **Open Screens** window as follows:

Figure 8.4: Metabot Designer window | Assets tab | Add Screen option

Under the **Open Screens** window, select the **Standard** option and click on the image of the application form to be captured as follows:

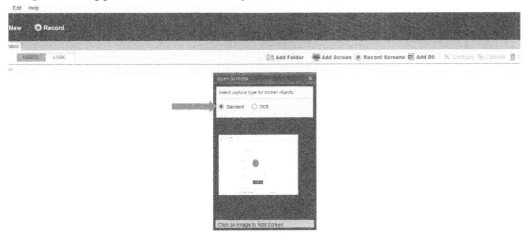

Figure 8.5: Open Screens window | Capture Image option

The captured screen will be visible under the **Assets** tab, and now, close the **Internet Explorer browser as follows**:

Figure 8.6: Captured screen under the Assets tab

Click on the **Logic** tab and under the **Logic** tab, click on **New Logic** button to open the **Workbench** window as follows:

Figure 8.7: Logic tab | New Logic option

> **This is an example of the Separation of UI and Logic, as screenshots are under the Assets tab and commands under the Logic tab.**

In the **Workbench** window, you will have access to the **Command Library** like in the task bot, with only networking commands like Active Directory, SNMP and so on, and obsolete commands like App Integration, Citrix Automation and so on, the Prompt and Web Recorder command being unavailable. All the other commands will work exactly the same way as in the task bot. The **Variable Manager** will have the same variable types as in the task bot. The **Workbench** will also have the screens/dll under the **Assets** tab visible on the right corner of the screen as follows:

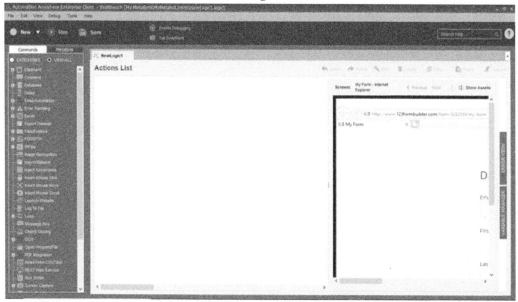

Figure 8.8: Workbench window for Metabot logic

The first step will be to take the **Begin Error Handling** subcommand under the **Error Handling** command. Use the **Excel** command and **Open Spreadsheet** subcommand and provide the path of the excel sheet from which the data has to be extracted and click on the **Save** button. Use the **Excel** command, **Get Cells** subcommand, and **Get All Cells** option and click on the **Save** button. Use the **Loop** command and **Each Row In An Excel Dataset** subcommand and click the **Save** button. These steps are the same as in the Excel Data Processing use case in *Chapter 6: Use Cases*. The metabot logic till now will look like as follows:

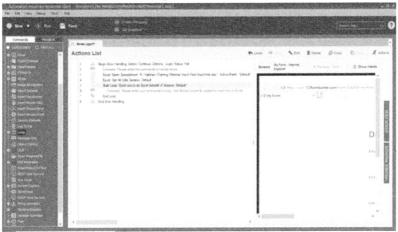

Figure 8.9: Metabot logic until now

Under the screen on the right side, use the scroll bar at the bottom to scroll and access the text box under **Email** and when the red outline appears around the text box click on it. In the Textbox1 window, under the **Select Action** option, provide **Set Text** as value and under the **Enter Text** option, provide $Excel Column(1)$ as the value through the **Insert Variable** window using the F2 key and click on the **Add** button as follows:

Figure 8.10: Object capture in screen and providing values for email textbox

This is an example of Offline Development, as you are able to capture the objects even if the application form has been closed.

Repeat the same process for the textboxes under the **First Name**, **Last Name** option, and dropdown list under the **Month**, **Day**, and **Year** option and the **Submit Form** button. After the **End Loop** statement, use the **Excel** command and **Close Spreadsheet** subcommand. Click on the **Save** button on the top and provide a meaningful logic name and then click on the **New** button to create a new task bot inside which the metabot logic will be called and executed as follows:

Figure 8.11: Complete metabot logic and New button to create a new task bot

The first step will be to take the **Begin Error Handling** subcommand under the **Error Handling** command. Use the **Web Recorder** command and **Open Browser** subcommand and pass the URL for the application form and click on the **Save** button. Click on the **Metabot** tab just above the **Command Library** and drag and drop the name of the metabot that you provided while creating the metabot under **Metabot Designer** as follows:

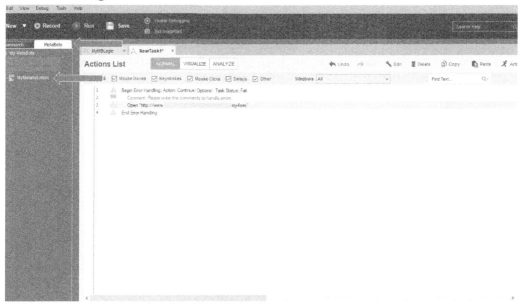

Figure 8.12: Metabot tab and metabot name

Select the name of the metabot logic that was just created and click on the **Save** button as follows:

Figure 8.13: Metabot logic selection

Use the **Web Recorder** command and **Close Browser** subcommand and click on the **Save** button as follows:

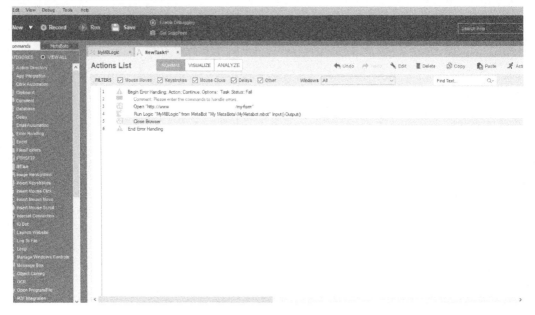

Figure 8.14: Complete task logic

Click on the **Save** button on the top and provide a meaningful task name and then click on the **Run** button to execute the bot and check the execution of the task bot which in turn will call and execute the metabot logic.

Now, the transfer of values between the metabot and task bot will be discussed. In the **Metabot Designer** window and under the **Logic** tab, click on the **New Logic** button to open the **Workbench** window. The first step will be to take the **Begin Error Handling** subcommand under the **Error Handling** command and then create the three variables of value type named mvFirstNum, mvSecondNum with **Parameter Type** as **Input** and mvResult with **Parameter Type** as None and null value for all the three variable, as the values will be transferred from the task bot to metabot logic in the first and second variable as follows:

Figure 8.15: *Task logic with the variables along with error handling command*

The naming convention for the **Metabot** variable is that it should use m as the prefix for the variable name, but for the further classification, you can use mv for a **Value** type variable, ml for a **List** type variable, ma for **Array** type variable, and mr for **Random type** variables.

Use the **Variable Operation** command and under the Specify variable option, select mvResult, and under the Specify value for the $Select variable$ option, provide the expression $mvFirstNum$ + $mvSecondNum$, using either *F2* for the **Insert Variable** window or directly writing it and then click on the **Save** button.

Use the **Message Box** command and provide the mvResult variable as the value and click on the **Save** button as follows:

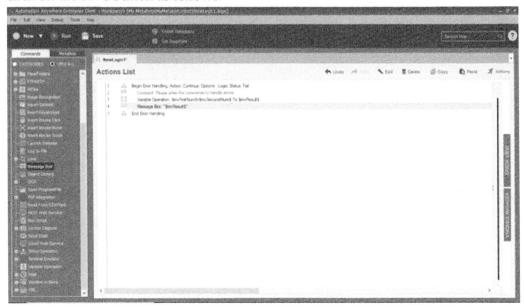

Figure 8.16: Complete metabot logic

Click on the **Save** button on the top and provide a meaningful logic name and then click on the **New** button to create a new task bot. The first step will be to take the **Begin Error Handling** subcommand under the **Error Handling** command and then create the two variables of the value type named vFirstNum and vSecondNum with a null value and use the **Prompt For Value** subcommand under the **Prompt** command to take the input from the user in the variables. Click on the **Metabot** tab just above the **Command Library** and drag and drop the name of the metabot under **Metabot Designer** and select the name of the metabot logic that was just created. Under the **Input Parameter** option map the variables by providing the vFirstNum variable next to mvFirstNum variable and vSecondNum variable next to mvSecondNum variable using the **Insert Variable** window and F2 key under the **Value** option as follows:

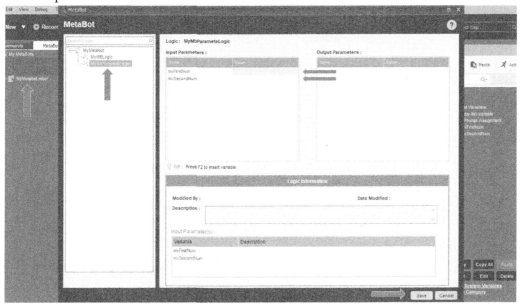

Figure 8.17: *Metabot window | Variable Mapping*

Click the **Save** button as follows:

Figure 8.18: *Complete task logic*

Click on the **Save** button on the top and provide a meaningful task name and then click on the **Run** button to execute the bot and check the execution of the task bot which in turn will call and execute metabot logic.

Now, the use of DLL will be discussed. A sample DLL code is as follows:

```
using System;
namespace AA_DLL_Utilities
{
  public class clsUtilities
  {
    public Object Add_Numbers(Int32 i, Int32 j)
    {
      return i+j;
    }
    public Object Multiply_Numbers(Int32 i, Int32 j)
    {
      return i*j;
    }
  }
}
```

In the **Metabot Designer** window and under the **Assets** tab, click on the **Add DLL** button to capture the d11 file whose classes are to be exposed and functions have to be executed as follows:

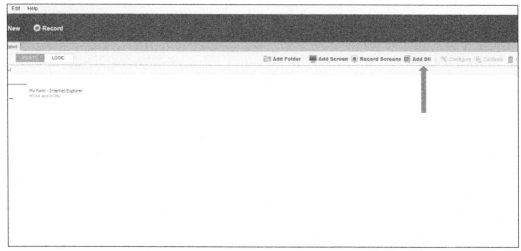

Figure 8.19: *Metabot Designer window | Assets tab | Add DLL option*

Under the **Logic** tab, click on the **New Logic** button to open the **Workbench** window. The first step will be to take the **Begin Error Handling** subcommand under the **Error Handling** command. Under the screen on the right side, use the **Next** and **Previous** button to access the dll file and then expand to access the class to be exposed and functions to be captured are visible as follows:

Figure 8.20: *Workbench window | Exposed DLL, class and functions*

Click on the method that you want to be executed at runtime to open the window to assign values to the parameters. Provide the values to the i and j parameters, and under the **Assign output** to variable option, provide **Prompt-Assignment** and click on the **Add** button as follows:

Figure 8.21: *Passing values to parameters*

Use the **Message Box** command and provide the **Prompt-Assignment** variable as the value and click on the **Save** button. Click on the **Save** button on the top and provide a meaningful logic name and then click on the **New** button to create a new task bot. The first step will be to take the **Begin Error Handling** subcommand under **the Error Handling** command and then click on the **Metabot** tab just above the **Command Library** and drag and drop the name of the metabot under **Metabot Designer** and select the name of the metabot logic that was just created and click on the **Save** button. Click on the **Save** button on the top and provide a meaningful task name and then click on the **Run** button to execute the bot and check the execution of the task bot which in turn will call and execute the metabot logic.

Now, the use of capturing the objects of applications running in *Citrix, SAP,* and *Remote* Desktop environments using the metabot will be discussed. Open the **Client Application** and click on the **MetaBots** option. Click on the **New Metabot** button on the right-hand corner to open the **New Metabot** window. In the **New Metabot** window, provide a name for the metabot under the **New Metabot** option, and under **Metabot Type** option, select **Application Specific** and select either the Citrix, SAP, or Remote environment whose objects are to be captured for automation and click the Create button to open the **Metabot Designer** window.

In the **Metabot Designer** window, under the **Assets** tab click on the **Add Screen** button to capture the application form whose objects are to be captured and open the Open **Screens** window. Under the **Open Screens** window, select the **OCR** option and click on the image of the application form to be captured as follows:

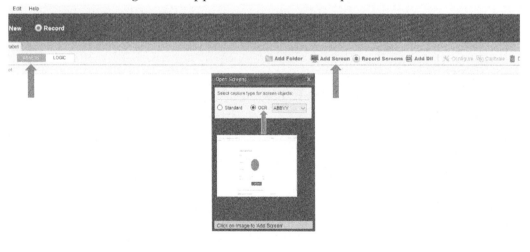

Figure 8.22: *Metabot Designer window | Add Screen option | Open Screens window | OCR option*

Click on the **Logic** tab, and under the **Logic** tab, click on the **New Logic** button to open the **Workbench** window. Under the **Screen** on the right side, use the scroll bar at the bottom to scroll and access the text box under **Email,** and this time, a blue outline will appear while capturing the object instead of red as seen in the following standard screen capture:

Figure 8.23: Objects in screen captured using OCR option selected with the blue outline

The rest of the logic creation and the calling of metabot into the task bot will remain the same as earlier.

> **The time to capture the screen will be higher and the metabot logic execution will be slower than the Standard capture.**

Conclusion

In this chapter, we discussed the metabot and the advantages provided by using the metabot. The capture of the objects using the Standard and OCR modes was discussed. The OCR mode is used for screen capture for objects to be captured of an application in Citrix, SAP, or Remote Desktop environment. The Offline development which is one of the biggest advantages provided by the metabot was also discussed during the chapter.

After the completion of the chapter, you can now create a Metabot using the Metabot Designer and capture the objects on the screen either using the Standard or the OCR modes.

In the next chapter, we will discuss the Recorders which are used to generate the task logic by capturing the steps being performed on the screen. The types of recorders available in Automation Anywhere are Screen, Web, and Smart Recorders.

Multiple choice questions

1. **Which option is selected under the Metabot Type in the New Metabot window when objects from multiple applications are to be selected?**

    a. Application-Specific

    b. All Application

    c. Multi-Application

    d. Meta Application

2. **Which mode is selected for the screen capture for objects to be captured of an application in Citrix, SAP, or Remote Desktop environment?**

    a. OCR

    b. Standard

    c. Citrix

    d. None of the above

3. **The new feature provided in Automation Anywhere v11 for objects to be captured of an application in Citrix, SAP, or Remote Desktop environment is _____.**

    a. AISense

    b. SenseAI

    c. Citrix AISense

    d. None of the above

Answer

1. *b*
2. *a*
3. *c*

CHAPTER 9
Recorders

Introduction

In this chapter, another approach to creating automation logic will be discussed which is to capture the operations on the screen and generate the automation logic for the process automation and are known as recorders.

Structure

In this chapter, we will discuss the following topics:

- Screen recorder
- Web recorder
- Smart recorder

Objectives

After completing this chapter, you should be able to:

- Understand how to use the screen recorder
- Understand how to use the web recorder
- Understand how to use the smart recorder

Recorders

The two approaches to create task bots are as follows:

- **Workbench**: You use the commands provided under command library and create an automation logic putting them sequentially one after the other as per the process requirement.

- **Recorders**: You perform the actions sequentially and manually of the process to be automated, and those actions will be captured by the recorders provided in Automation Anywhere to generate the automation logic. The generated recording will have the same commands provided under command library.

Recorders are of the following three types:

- **Screen**: It is used for capturing actions being performed on the desktop applications. The commands generated are: **Insert Keystrokes**, **Insert Mouse Click**, **Insert Mouse Move**, and **Insert Mouse Scroll**. As the **Insert Mouse Click**, **Insert Mouse Move**, and **Insert Mouse Scroll** are commands which are dependent on the coordinate position of the objects on the screen; hence, the screen recorder is the least reliable of the recorders.

- **Web**: As the name suggests, this recorder is used to capture the data from the web applications. The three types of data that can be captured using the web recorder are as follows:

    o **Table Data**: Extract the data from an Internet Explorer table.

    o **Regular Data**: Extracts a single value data from the web page.

    o **Pattern Data**: Extracts the data of the objects presented in a similar layout like products on the e-commerce websites.

- **Smart**: This recorder is used to capture actions being performed on both the desktop and web applications. It is because the command generated is **Object Cloning** that can capture objects of both desktop and web applications.

Screen recorder

The first recorder that we will see in action is a screen recorder, and to make it reliable and scalable only the **Insert Keystrokes** command will be used. Create a text file with the name `Attendance.txt` and use F5 to register the timestamp in the text file and then save the file directly in the D or E drive, so that it has a shorter path to provide while opening the file.

Open the Client Application and click on the the the down arrow next to the **Record** button and select the **Screen Recorder** option and then, click on the **Record** button to start recording as follows:

Figure 9.1: *Screen Recorder selection*

Open the **Run** window using the keys combination, Win + r as follows:

Figure 9.2: *Screen recorder | Win + r*

Provide the path of the `Attendance.txt` file inside the **Run** window and provide the path slowly so that the recorder can identify the keys pressed correctly and then, press the Enter key to open the file.

In the following figure, write the full path and do not capture the path from the autocomplete coming at the bottom:

Figure 9.3: Screen recorder | Run window

In the `Attendance.txt` file, press the keys combination Ctrl + End to move the cursor to the end of the content as follows:

Figure 9.4: Screen recorder | Ctrl + End

Next, press the *Enter* key to move the cursor to the new line as follows:

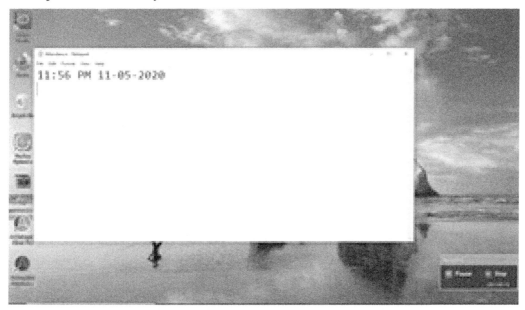

Figure 9.5: *Screen recorder | Enter*

Next, press the F5 key to enter the new timestamp as follows:

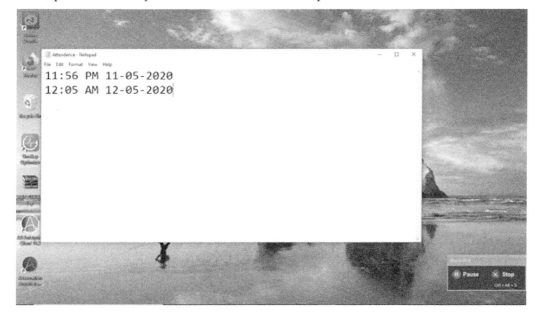

Figure 9.6: *Screen recorder | F5*

Now, press the keys combination *Ctrl + S* to save the content and *Alt + F4* to close the file as follows:

Figure 9.7: Screen recorder | Ctrl + s and Alt + F4

Click on the **Stop** button at the bottom-right corner of the screen and provide the name to save the recording and then, click on the **Save** button as follows:

Figure 9.8: Screen recorder | Stop button

The recording has been captured, and now, we can open the recording in `Workbench` using the `Edit` button at the top of the **Client Application** as follows:

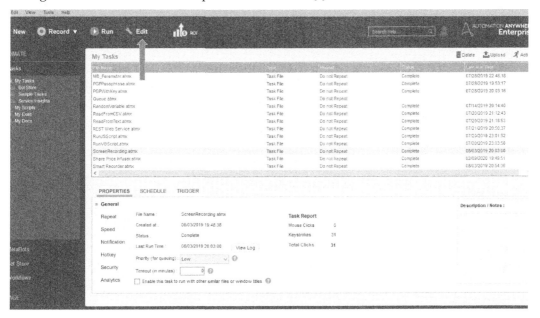

Figure 9.9: *Client Application | Edit button*

Remove all the other command apart from the **Insert Keystrokes** command and change the Delay to 500 milliseconds, as the time taken to perform each action during recording is captured by the **Screen Recorder** as follows:

Figure 9.10: *Complete task logic*

Click on the **Save** button on the top and then click on the **Run** button to execute the bot and check the execution of the task bot generated by using the screen recorder.

Web recorder

The next recorder in action is the web recorder, and the first extraction will be of the table data. Open the **Client Application** and click on the down arrow next to the **Record** button and select the **Web Recorder** option and then click on the **Record** button to start recording. Under the **URL** option, provide the URL of the website from which you want to capture the data of the table and click on the **Next** button as follows:

Figure 9.11: Web Recorder

Click on the **Ok** button under the **Web Recorder Tip** wndow as follows:

Figure 9.12: Web Recorder Tip window

Click on the **Extract Table** button on the bottom-right of the screen as follows:

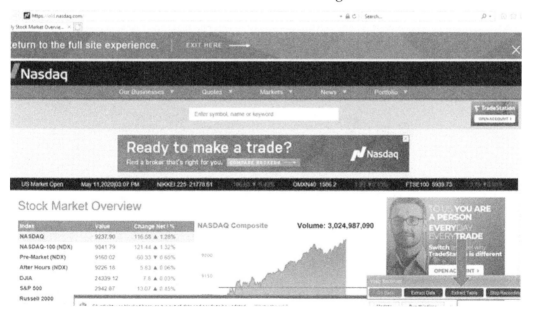

Figure 9.13: Web Recorder | Extract table option

Move the cursor to the table from which the data has to be captured and wait for the green border to appear around the table that signals that the recorder has identified the table to capture the data and then, click on the table for the data to be captured by the recorder as follows:

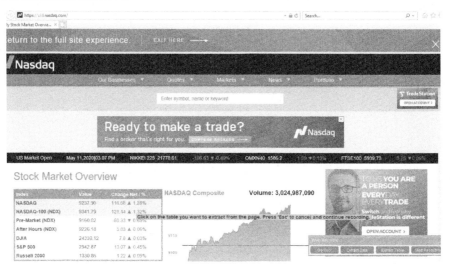

Figure 9.14: *Web Recorder | green border around the table*

Check **The table** spans across multiple pages checkbox if the data of the table to be extracted is on multiple pages, and then, click on the **Capture** button to capture the **Next** button on the web page that denotes that till the time the **Next** button will be active on the table while running the bot it will keep capturing the data from the multiple pages of the table. If the data is only on a single page as in this case, then click on the **Next** button as follows:

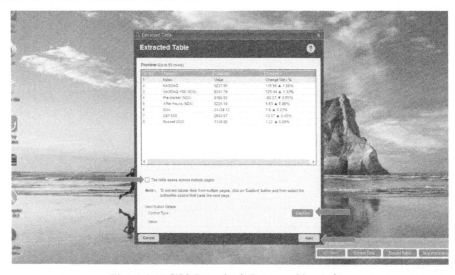

Figure 9.15: *Web Recorder | Extract table window*

Provide the path of the CSV file in which the extracted data will be saved under the **Extract Table Data to a csv file** option, and then, click on the **Finish** button as follows:

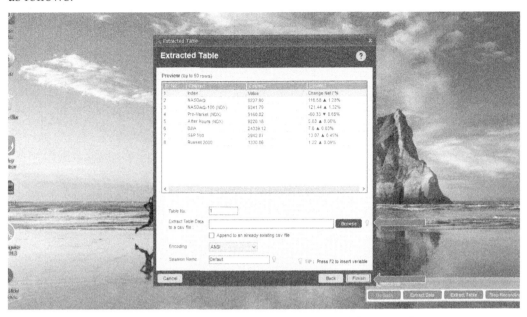

Figure 9.16: Web Recorder | Extract table window | file save options

Click on the **Stop Recording** button at the bottom-right corner of the screen to stop the recording as follows:

Figure 9.17: Web Recorder | Stop Recording

Provide the name to save the recording under the **Filename** option and click on the **Save** button as follows:

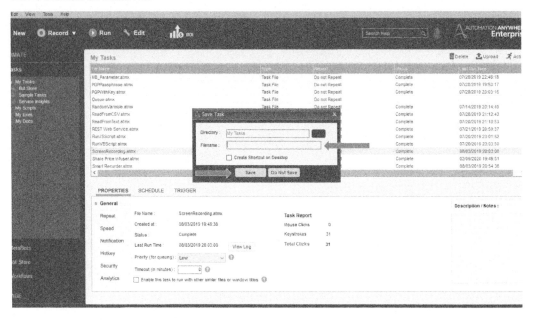

Figure 9.18: *Web recorder | Save the recording*

The recording has been captured, and now, open the recording in **Workbench** using the **Edit** button at the top of client application as follows:

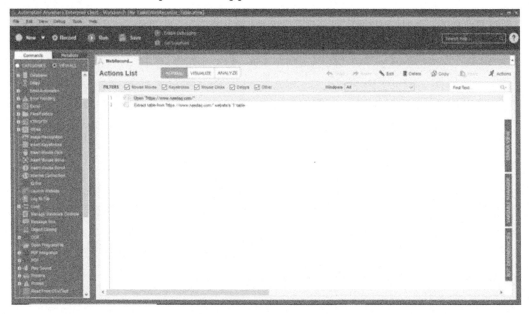

Figure 9.19: *Complete task logic*

Click on the **Save** button on the top, and then, click on the **Run** button to execute the bot and check the execution of the task bot generated by using the web recorder. The recorder in action again is the web recorder and the extraction will be of a single value data which is known as Regular data. Open the client application and click on the down arrow next to the **Record** button and select **Web Recorder** option, and then, click on the **Record** button to start the recording.

Under the **URL** option, provide the URL of the website from which you want to capture the data of the table and click on the **Next** button as follows:

Figure 9.20: Web Recorder

Click on the **Ok** button under the **Web Recorder Tip** window as follows:

Figure 9.21: Web Recorder Tip window

Click on the **Extract Data** button on the bottom-right of the screen as follows:

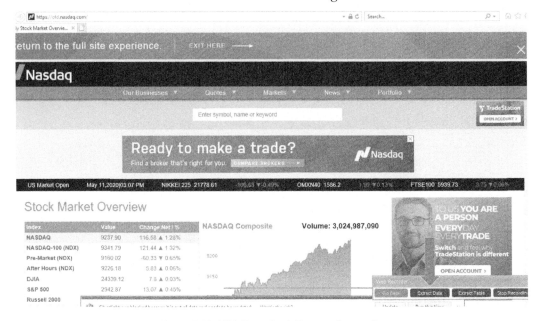

Figure 9.22: *Web Recorder | Extract data option*

Under the **Extract Data Option** window, select the **Regular** data option and click on the **Next** button as follows:

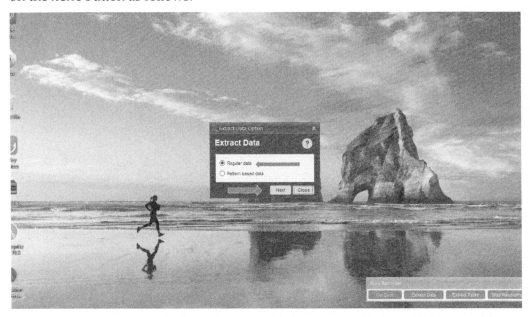

Figure 9.23: *Web Recorder | Extract data | regular data option*

Move the cursor to the value from which the data has to be captured and wait for the green border to appear around the value that signals that the recorder has identified the value which is to be captured, and then, click on the value to be captured by the recorder as follows:

Figure 9.24: *Web Recorder | green border around the value*

Under the **Extract Data** window, check if the correct value has been captured under the **HTML Control Value** option and assign the captured value to the **Prompt-Assignment** variable next to the **Extract control value to a variable** option and click on the **Save** button as follows:

Figure 9.25: *Extract data window options*

Click on the **Stop Recording** button at the bottom-right corner of the screen to stop the recording as follows:

Figure 9.26: Web Recorder | Stop Recording

Provide the name to save the recording under the **Filename** option and click on the **Save** button as follows:

Figure 9.27: Web recorder | Save recording

The recording has been captured, and now, open the recording in **Workbench** using the **Edit** button at the top of client application. Add a **Message Box** command at Line 3 and provide the **Prompt-Assignment** variable under the **Please enter message to show to the user** option as follows:

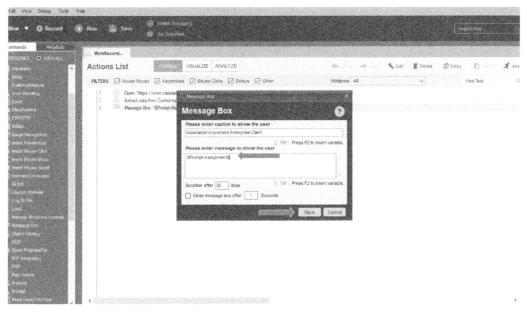

Figure 9.28: Web recording | Message box command

Click on the **Save** button in the **Message Box** window as follows:

Figure 9.29: Complete task logic

Click on the **Save** button on the top, and then, click on the **Run** button to execute the bot and check the execution of the task bot generated by using the web recorder. The recorder in action again is the web recorder and the extraction will be of the pattern-based data. Open the client application and click on the down arrow next to the **Record** button and select the **Web Recorder** option, and then, click on the **Record** button to start the recording.

Under the **URL** option, provide the URL of the website from which you want to capture the data of the table and click on the **Next** button as follows:

Figure 9.30: Web Recorder

Click on the **Ok** button under the **Web Recorder Tip** window as follows:

Figure 9.31: Web Recorder Tip window

Click on the **Extract Data** button on the bottom-right of the screen as follows:

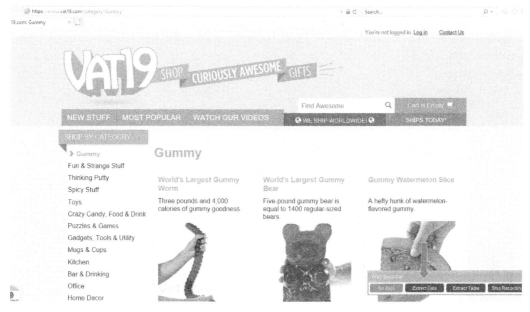

Figure 9.32: *Web Recorder | Extract data option*

Under the **Extract Data Option** window, select the **Regular data** option and click on the **Next** button as follows:

Figure 9.33: *Web Recorder | Extract data | pattern-based data option*

The values that are to be extracted for all the products are the name of the product, description of the product, and image of the product. If the names of the product are to be captured, then the name of the first and second product will have to be selected one after the other to establish the pattern. Move the cursor over the first product name and wait for the green border to appear around it, and now, click on it as follows:

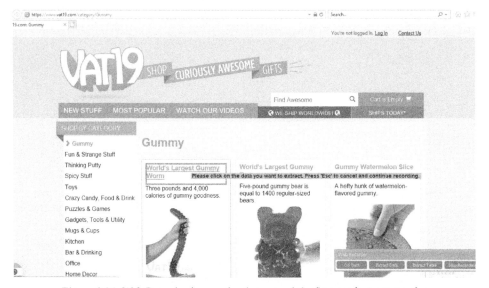

Figure 9.34: Web Recorder | green border around the first product name value

Click on the **Capture** button on the dialog box that appears after we click on the value as follows:

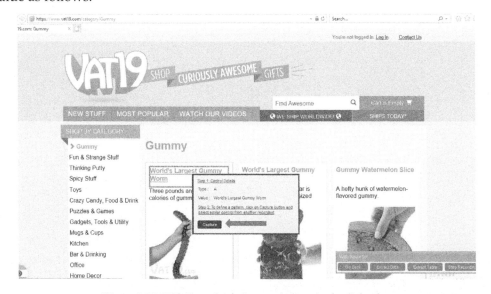

Figure 9.35: Web Recorder | Capture button in the dialog box

Move the cursor now over the second product name and wait for the green border to appear around it, and now, click on it as follows:

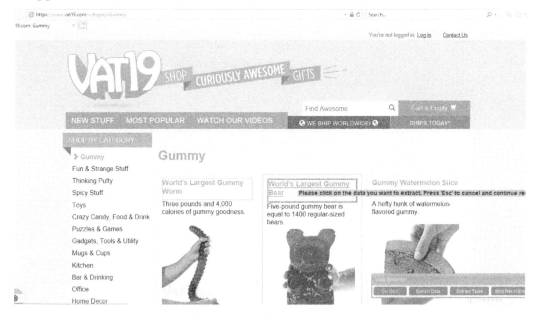

Figure 9.36: *Web Recorder | green border around the second product name value*

Under the **Extract Data Fields** window, provide the name for the column next to the **Enter Column Name** option and click on the **Save** button as follows:

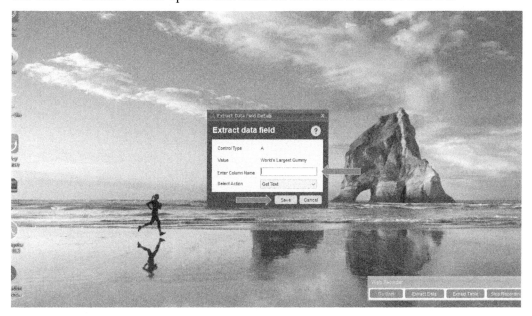

Figure 9.37: *Web Recorder | Extract data Fields window*

Click on the **Add** button under the **Extract Multiple Data** window and capture the description and image fields for the products following the same process used for capturing product names as follows:

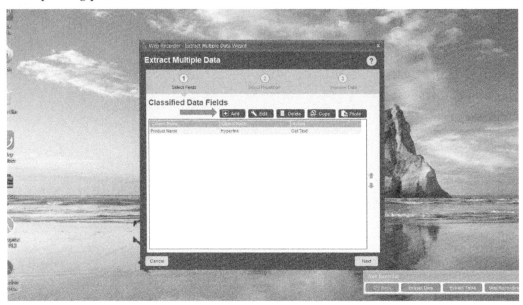

Figure 9.38: Web Recorder | Extract Multiple Data window

Once all the three fields have been captured, click on the **Next** button under the **Extract Multiple Data** window as follows:

Figure 9.39: Web Recorder | Extract Multiple Data | Next button

Check **The table** spans across multiple pages checkbox if the data to be extracted is on multiple pages, and then, click on the **Capture** button to capture the **Next** button on the web page which denotes that till the time the **Next** button will be active on the web page while running the bot, it will keep capturing the product data from the multiple pages. If the data is only on a single page as in this case, then click on the **Next** button under the **Extract Multiple Data** window as follows:

Figure 9.40: Web Recorder | Extract Multiple Data | Next button

Click on the **Preview Data** button if you want to preview the values that has been captured. Provide the path of the CSV file in which the captured data will be saved next to the **Extract data to a csv file** option by clicking the **Browse** button and provide the path of the folder in which the product images will be saved next to the **Extract images to folder** option by clicking the **Browse** button, and now, click on the **Finish** button as follows:

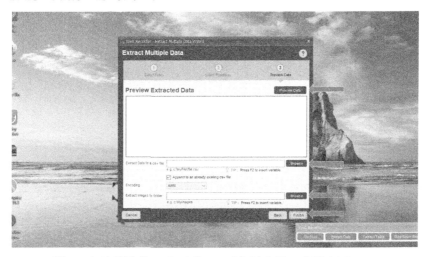

Figure 9.41: Web Recorder | Extract Multiple Data | Finish button

Click on the **Stop Recording** button at the bottom-right corner of the screen to stop the recording as follows:

Figure 9.42: Web Recorder | Stop Recording

Provide the name to save the recording under the **Filename** option and click on the **Save** button as follows:

Figure 9.43: Web recorder | Save the recording

The recording has been captured, and now, open the recording in **Workbench** using the **Edit** button at the top of client application as follows:

Figure 9.44: *Complete task logic*

Click on the **Save** button on the top, and then, click on the **Run** button to execute the bot and check the execution of the task bot generated by using the web recorder.

Smart recorder

The next recorder in action is the smart recorder. Open the **Control Panel,** as we will be capturing objects in the Control Panel using the smart recorder. Open the client application and click on the down arrow next to the **Record** button and select the **Web Recorder** option and then click on the **Record** button to start the recording as follows:

Figure 9.45: Smart Recorder

Under the **Select window** option, select **Control Panel** and click on the **Start** button in the Recorder window as follows:

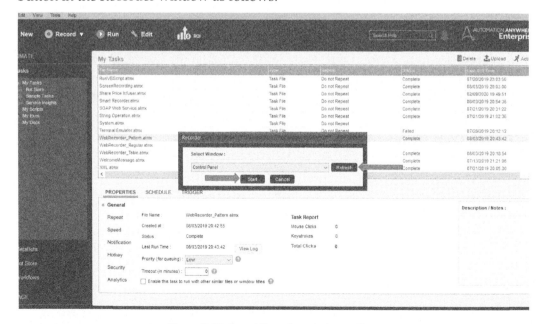

Figure 9.46: Smart Recorder window options

Click on the **System and Security** option under the **Control Panel** window as follows:

Figure 9.47: *Control Panel | System and Security*

Click on the **Power Options** option under the **System and Security** window as follows:

Figure 9.48: *System and Security | Power Options*

Move the cursor to the **Screen Brightness** option under the **Power Options** window as follows:

Figure 9.49: *Power Options | Screen Brightness*

Change the brightness of the screen using the **Screen Brightness** option as follows:

Figure 9.50: *Change brightness of the screen*

Click on the **Stop** button at the bottom-right corner of the screen and provide the name to save the recording and click on the **Save** button as follows:

Figure 9.51: *Smart recorder | Stop button*

The recording has been captured, and now, open the recording in **Workbench** using the **Edit** button at the top of client application as follows:

Figure 9.52: *Complete task logic*

Click on the **Save** button on the top, and then, click on the **Run** button to execute the bot and change the screen brightness to the original setting and go to the **Control Panel** home window and check the execution of the task bot generated by using the smart recorder.

Conclusion

In this chapter, we discussed another approach to create the task bots that are recorders. Recorders are of three types, namely, screen, web, and smart recorders. The screen recorder is used for desktop applications; web recorder is used for web applications, and it can capture three types of data from the web application, table data, single value, and pattern-based data. A smart recorder can be used for both the desktops as well as web applications.

After completing this chapter, you can capture the steps being performed on the screen using the screen recorder for the desktop applications, capture data from web applications using the web recorder, and capture the steps from the desktop or web application using the smart recorder.

In the next chapter, we will discuss the lockers and credential variables that are used to save secure information. The credential variables can be accessed by the developer, but the value cannot be seen by the developer during the bot development.

Multiple choice questions

1. Which recorder captures the time taken to perform each action during the recording of the task?

   a.   Smart

   b.   Web

   c.   Screen

   d.   None of the above

2. Which recorder provides the option to capture the regular data?

   a.   Screen

   b.   Web

   c.   Smart

   d.   None of the above

3. Which recorder generates Object Cloning command to capture the objects during the recording of the task?

   a.   Smart

   b.   Web

   c.   Screen

   d.   None of the above

Answer

1. *c*
2. *b*
3. *a*

CHAPTER 10
Credential Variables

Introduction

In this chapter, you will learn about the lockers and credential variables. The credential variables are used to store sensitive information that can be used by the developers during the bot creation but cannot be viewed. The credential variables should be stored inside the lockers as only the credential variables inside a locker are accessible to the developers.

Structure

In this chapter, we will discuss the following topics:

- Creation of locker
- Creation of credential variable
- Consuming credential variable

Objectives

After completing this chapter, you should be able to:

- Understand how to create a locker
- Understand how to create the credential variable
- Understand how to consume credential variable

Credential variable

The credential variables are used to store sensitive information that the developers can only use for the bot creation but cannot view it during the development of the bot. Assume there is a process to be automated in which the login credentials of the Project Manager are to be used for logging in to the application and then used to perform some task. Now, the Project Manager would not like to share his credentials with the developer for some security reasons. So, to overcome this challenge, a credential variable can be created in the Web Control Room in which the Project Manager can save the login details that can be accessed by the developer for developing the bot but cannot access the login detail values. The credential variables are created inside the lockers and to access the locker and the variables, the developer should have a user-defined role that will be assigned as the locker consumer and credential variable consumer.

The first step would be to create a user-created role and assign it to the developer. Login into the Web Control Room using the Web Control Room Admin login credentials and select the **Roles** tab under the **Administration** tab and click on the **Create Role** icon on the right-hand side top corner as follows:

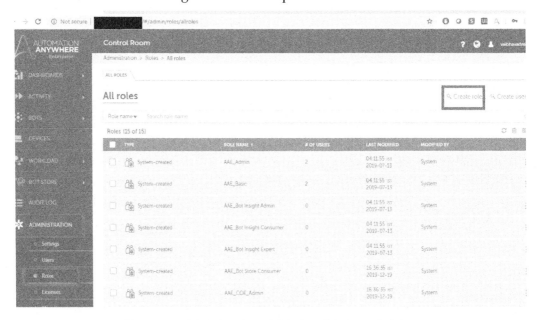

Figure 10.1: *Administration tab | Roles tab | Create Role icon*

Under the **Role** name option, provide a unique name for the role that you are creating, and by selecting the checkboxes, you can provide access to the user to whom this role is assigned to specific tabs like Dashboard, Activity, and so on and specific actions under the tabs and after selecting the access permissions and click on the **Create Role** button at the right-hand side top corner as follows:

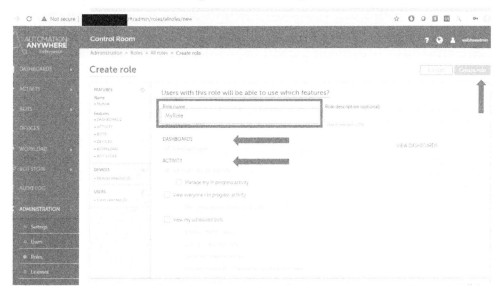

Figure 10.2: User-created role creation option

You can check the role that you just created under the **Roles** tab and it will be provided in the list after the System created roles as follows:

Figure 10.3: User-created role under Roles tab

Under the **Administration** tab and **Users** tab, click on the three dots button at the last of the user that you had earlier created with the Bot Creator license and click on the pencil icon and **Edit User** option as follows:

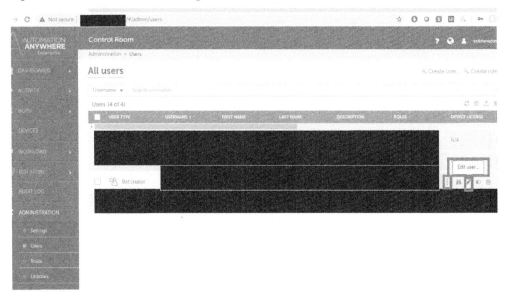

Figure 10.4: Edit User option under Roles tab

Under the **Select role** option on the **Edit User page,** select the just created role and click on the button with the right arrow sign to select the role and then scroll up as follows:

Figure 10.5: Edit User | Select Role option

Click on the **Save Changes** button as follows:

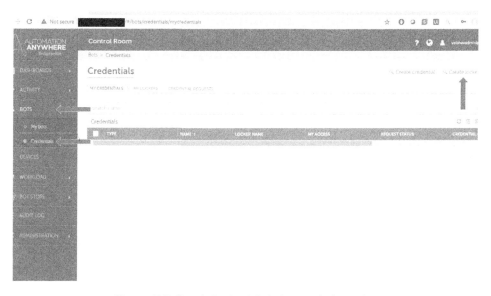

Figure 10.6: *Edit User | Save changes button*

Create another user with the **None** license and then select the role of AAE_Admin and AAE_LockerAdmin and login to the Web Control Room using the credentials of the Admin user that you just created as only a user with the locker admin role can create a locker.

Select the **Credentials** tab under **Bots** tab and click on the **Create locker** button as follows:

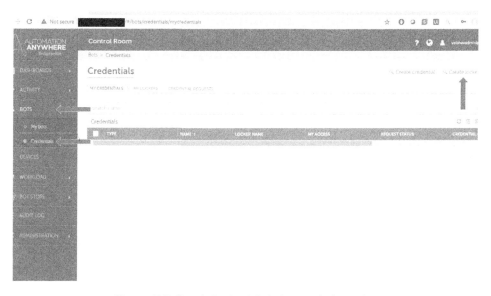

Figure 10.7: *Bots | Credentials | Create a locker option*

Under the **Locker name** option, provide a unique name for the locker and click on the **Next** button to provide the **Owner**, **Manager**, **Participant**, and **Consumer** for the locker by clicking the **Next** button. The owner will be the user who is creating the locker. You can add other owners as well. The manager and the participant are optional. Under the **Consumer** option, select the user-created role and click on the right arrow button and then click on the **Create locker** button at the top as follows:

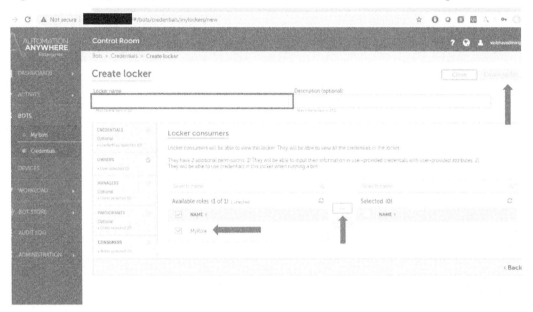

Figure 10.8: Create locker options

Permissions of each of them are listed as follows:

- **Owner:** As a Locker administrator, you can remove the owners. However, every locker should have at least one owner. Therefore, if there is only one owner and it is disabled, add another owner, and then the disabled owner will become enabled.

- **Manager:** The locker managers have all the permissions that owners do except they cannot add other owners, managers, or participants.

- **Participant:** The locker participants will be able to view this locker. They will be able to add (but not remove) their credentials to this locker. They will be able to see their credentials, but no other credentials, that are in the locker.

- **Consumer:** The locker consumers will be able to view this locker. They will be able to view all the credentials in the locker. They have two following additional permissions:

  1. They will be able to input their information in the user-provided credentials with the user-provided attributes.

2. They will be able to use the credentials in this locker when running a bot.

Select **Credentials** tab under **Bots** tab and click on the **Create locker** button as follows:

Figure 10.9: *Bots | Credentials | Create credential option*

Under the **Credential name** option, provide a unique name of the credential variable. Select the locker that you just created under the **General** option and the right arrow button to attach the variable as part of the selected locker. Under the **Attributes** option, provide the **Attribute** name value as loginid, and then select **Standard** and provide the value and select the **Masked** option. Click on the **Plus (+)** icon at the bottom and provide the **Attribute** name value as password and then select **Standard** and provide the value. Now, select **Masked and Password** option and click on the **Create credential** button at the top as follows:

Figure 10.10: *Create credential options*

Open the Client Application and create a new task bot in **Workbench**. Open a web application with the login page in the internet explorer browser. Use the **Object Cloning** command, and under the **Selected Window** option, select the internet explorer window and click on the **Capture** button to capture the textbox for providing the login id. Under the **Actions** option, select the **Set Text** option, and under the Text to Set option, press F2 to open the **Insert Variable** window and then double click on the locker name to open the **Select Credential** window. Under the **Credential Name** option, select the name of your credential variable, and under the **Attribute Name** option, select the login id attribute and click on the **Ok** button as follows:

Figure 10.11: Object Cloning command

Click on the **Save** button on the **Object Cloning** window as follows:

Figure 10.12: Object Cloning | Text to Set | Select Credential window

Repeat the same process to provide the password attribute for developing the bot. The process can be automated now with the security of the login values being maintained using the credential variables.

> The credential variables can also be used as global variables, as they are available to all the users who have been provided the consumer permission.

Conclusion

In this chapter, we discussed the credential variables and the security advantages provided by using the credential variables during the development of the bot. We also discussed the user-created role, locker creation, and creating the credential variables with multiple attributes and then consuming the credential variable.

After completing this chapter, you can now create the locker and credential variable in the Web Control Room and can consume them during the bot creation in the client application as a developer provided you have the requisite privileges.

In the next chapter, we will discuss IQ bots that have the cognitive capabilities and use Computer Vision, **Natural Language Processing** (**NLP**), fuzzy logic, and **Machine Learning (ML)** to process the documents.

Multiple choice questions

1. **The user, with which role, can create the Credential locker?**

    a. AAE_Admin

    b. AAE_QueueAdmin

    c. AAE_PoolAdmin

    d. AAE_LockerAdmin

2. **A developer can only _____ the credential variable attribute but cannot _____ the value of credential variable attribute during the bot development.**

    a. view, access

    b. access, view

    c. view, see

    d. None of the above

Answer

1. *d*

2. *b*

CHAPTER 11
IQ Bots

Introduction

In this chapter, we will discuss the IQ bots using which the cognitive capabilities can be added in the process automation. Different technologies like Computer Vision, fuzzy logic, **natural language processing** (**NLP**), and **machine learning** (**ML**) in the background to equip the IQ bots with cognitive capabilities. Training the IQ bots is exactly like]teaching a kid.

Structure

In this chapter, we will discuss the following topics:

- Development of the IQ Bots
- Working of the IQ Bots
- Using the IQ Bots

Objectives

After completing this chapter, you should be able to:

- Understand how to develop the IQ Bots with learning instances that can help to train your bots
- Understand how to use or call the IQ Bots in your automation

IQ Bots

Cognitive capabilities can be added using the IQ bots for process automation and ease the development of bots for a lot of processes whose automation would be pretty difficult without the use of the IQ bots.

According to Automation Anywhere, the IQ bot combines the power of RPA with AI technologies such as Computer Vision, **natural language processing (NLP)**, fuzzy logic, and machine learning (ML) to automatically classify, extract, and validate the information from the business documents and emails.

Let us say there is a business process in which the data has to be extracted from multiple invoices sent by different vendors. The issue with invoices is that different vendors can send invoices in different formats. Imagine, some vendors might write the Invoice Number as Invoice # in their invoices. Some of them might write Invoice numbers as Invoice No and some might write the Invoice number as Invoice Number. Some might write the Invoice number at the top of the invoice or the bottom or at the left section of the invoice or to the right section of the invoice. Now, there are multiple variations for the same field to be captured with no fixed structure.

In the precedingly discussed scenario, we can use the IQ bots. We can train the IQ bot to learn and identify that the Invoice Number, Invoice No, and Invoice # are the same field with a different variation.

A lot of different types of business documents can be processed using the IQ bots, which have issues as discussed earlier. If you are using Automation Anywhere Community Edition, the documents that can be processed are as follows:

- Bank Statement
- Credit Memo
- Invoices
- Purchase Orders
- Utility Bills
- Custom (Other)

If you are using Automation Anywhere Enterprise Edition, the documents that can be processed in addition to those available in Automation Anywhere Community Edition are as follows:

- Automobile Insurance Claim
- Bill of Exchange
- Bill of Lading
- Billing Statement
- Contracts
- Council Tax
- Credit Card Statement

- Electricity Bills
- Explanation of Benefits
- Facturas (Spanish Invoices)
- Health Insurance Claim (1500)
- Health Insurance Claim (UB 04)
- Inspection Certificate
- Mortgage Statement
- Motor Insurance Certificate
- Nota Fiscal (Brazilian Invoices)
- Packing Lists
- Pay Stubs
- Standard Settlement Instructions
- Telephone Bill
- Transport Document
- US 1040 Form
- US W4 Form

There are four following stages to create your IQ bot to process the documents:

- **Upload:** The business documents are uploaded for the creation of an IQ bot learning instance.

- **Classify:** The IQ bot will distribute the documents into different groups based on the differentiation in the document structure. The invoices that have Invoice # as the Invoice Number field will be classified in a separate group, and the invoices with Invoice No as the Invoice Number field will be classified into a separate group.

- **Train:** Review the mapped fields and train the bot for corrections to improve the data extraction accuracy.

- **Production:** After the completion of the IQ bot training, set it to the production mode so that it is available to be used inside the task bot for real-time document processing.

In this book, Automation Anywhere Community Edition is being used for the IQ bot learning as the IQ bot is a licensed product and is not available to everyone. Automation Anywhere Community Edition provides a free IQ bot environment with a limited number of learning instances. We will be processing invoices using the IQ bot. The sample invoices are as follows:

The following is the sample first invoice:

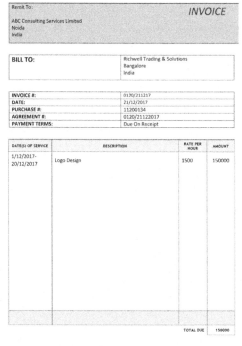

Figure 11.1: *Sample Invoice 1*

The following is the sample second invoice:

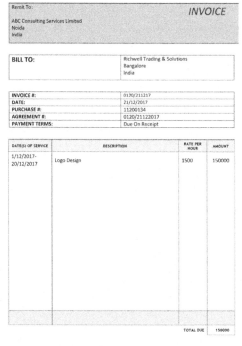

Figure 11.2: *Sample Invoice 2*

The following is the sample third invoice:

Remit To:

ABC Consulting Services Limited
Noida
India

INVOICE

BILL TO:	HoneyMax Designers Mumbai India

INVOICE #:	0122/211251
DATE:	22/12/2017
PURCHASE #:	11200145
AGREEMENT #:	0122/22122017
PAYMENT TERMS:	Due On Receipt

DATE(S) OF SERVICE	DESCRIPTION	RATE PER HOUR	AMOUNT
11/12/2017-15/12/2017	Consumer Survey Analysis	2000	100000
		TOTAL DUE	100000

SIGNATURE: ABC Consulting Services Ltd

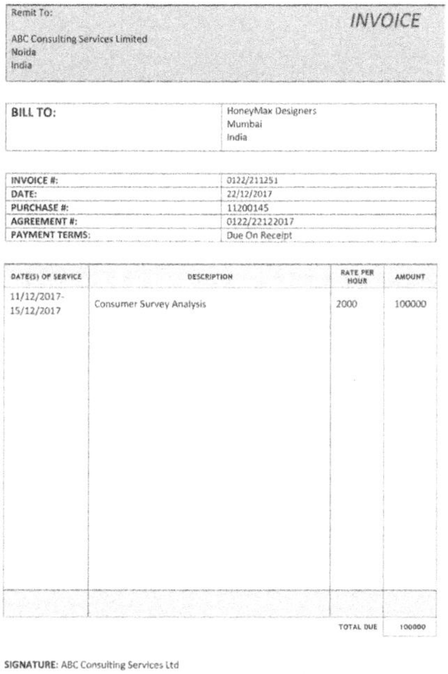

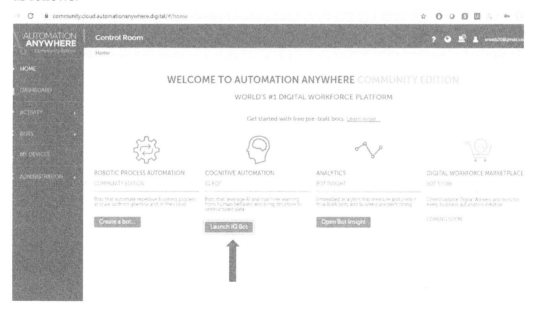

Figure 11.3: *Sample Invoice 3*

Invoice 1 is in different format, and *Invoice 2* and *Invoice 3* are in different formats. So, they will be classified under separate groups. The first task will be to login to Automation Anywhere Community Edition and click on the **`Launch IQ Bot`** button as follows:

Figure 11.4: *Automation Anywhere Community Edition window for launching IQ bot*

Click on the **Get Started** button on the IQ bot home page as follows:

Figure 11.5: IQ bot home page

Let the page load and wait for some time for the **New Instance** button to activate and then click on it as follows:

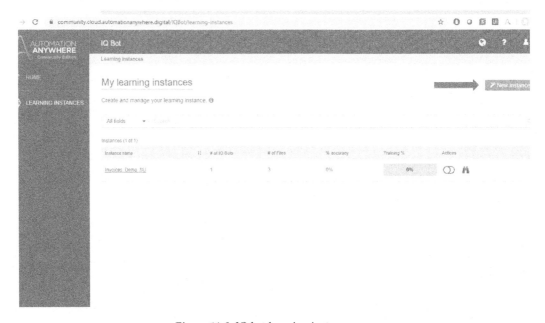

Figure 11.6: IQ bot learning instance page

Upload

Under the **General Information** header, provide the name for learning instance under the **Instance Name** option, and under the **Document Type** option, select **Invoices**. You can select the document language under the **Primary language of document** option. By default, it is **English**. The other options provided are **German**, **French**, **Spanish**, and **Italian**. Upload your invoices under the **Upload Documents** options by clicking the **Browse** button. If you do not have sample invoices, you can click on the **Download Sample Documents** button and then upload those invoices as follows:

Figure 11.7: New instance page options

Under the **Fields to Extract** header, select the fields that you want to extract from the documents under the **Common Form Fields and Common table/ repeated** section fields option. You can select from the extra pre-defined fields as well by clicking on the two down arrow icon at the right corner. Once the fields to be extracted are captured, click on the **Create instance and analyze** button as follows:

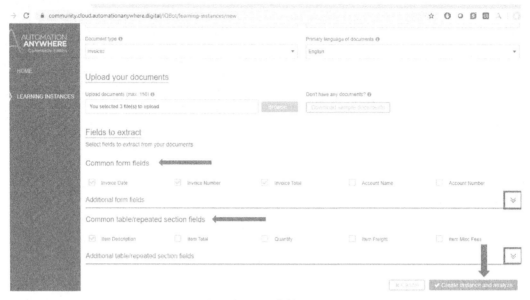

Figure 11.8: New instance field extraction options

Classify

The IQ bot will now analyze the document and classify them into separate groups for data extraction as follows:

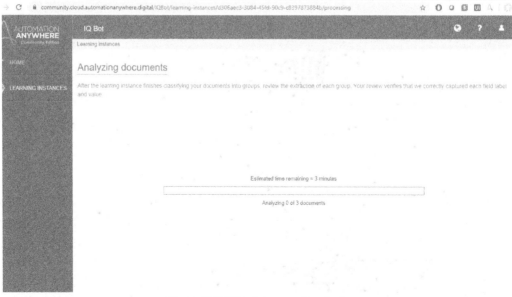

Figure 11.9: IQ bot document analysis

Train

The IQ bot will now open the review page. Check whether each of the fields has correct data extracted or not by reviewing the data under the **Field** header. You can also check the extracted data by clicking on the **See extraction results** button. If all the fields have been captured correctly, click on **Save** and go to the next group button as follows:

Figure 11.10: IQ bot document review

If any field is not captured correctly as is the case with the **Description** field, then click on the **Draw** button and select the area around the value to be captured to train your bot to extract the correct value and click on **Save** and go to the next group button as follows:

Figure 11.11: IQ bot document field extraction review

Click on the **Save** button to move on to the next document group review as follows:

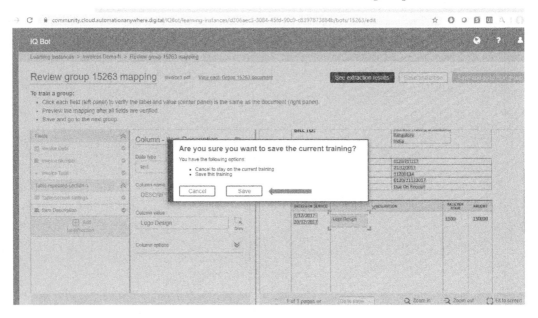

Figure 11.12: *IQ bot next document group*

Review all the document groups as earlier and click on the **Save** and close button to mark the completion of the document review and click on the **Save** button as follows:

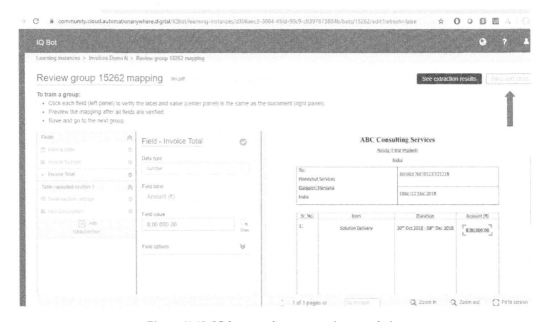

Figure 11.13: *IQ bot next document review completion*

Production

Click on the **Set to production** button so that the IQ bot can be called inside the task bot and used for document processing as follows:

Figure 11.14: IQ bot production

Click on the **Yes**, send to production button to confirm as follows:

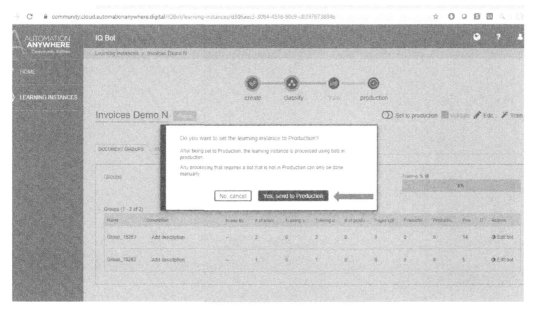

Figure 11.15: IQ bot production confirmation

The IQ bot development has now been completed, and the bot now is in the production as follows:

Figure 11.16: IQ bot in production

Calling IQ Bots

Login to the client application using the credentials of the Automation Anywhere Community Edition user and open a new **Workbench** window. The first step will be to take the **Begin Error Handling** subcommand under the **Error Handling** command. The task logic should look like as follows till here:

Figure 11.17: Task logic with error handling command

Use the **Loop** command and **Each File In A Folder** subcommand and provide the path of the folder in which the invoices have been kept under the **Select Folder** option by clicking on the **Browse** button and then click on the **Save** button as follows:

Figure 11.18: Loop command | Each File In A Folder subcommand

Use the **IQ Bot** command inside the **Loop** command. Under the **Select Learning Instance** option, choose the name of the IQ bot learning instance created previously. Under the **Select Source File** option, select the files inside the folder in which the invoices are kept and click on the **Save** button. You can copy the path of the output files with **Successful and Invalid extraction of data** from the provided documents as follows:

Figure 11.19: IQ Bot command

Click on the **Save** button on the top and provide a meaningful task name and then click on the **Run** button to execute the bot and check the result in the output files.

Conclusion

In this chapter, we discussed the IQ bot, the creation of IQ bot learning instances, and to call the IQ bot inside the task bot. We learned about the different types of documents that can be processed inside Automation Anywhere Community Edition and Automation Anywhere Enterprise Edition. We learned about the four stages of the IQ bot learning instance creation which are Upload, Classify, Train, and Production.

After completing this chapter, we can now create an IQ bot learning instance using the four stages that are Upload, Classify, Train, and Production. Once the IQ bot has been created, we can then call them in our bot logic.

In the next chapter, we will discuss the workflows that provide a graphical interface to create our process flow execution based on the fulfillment of the specified conditions.

Multiple choice questions

1. **Which document type is available for the IQ bot processing under Automation Anywhere Community Edition?**
   a. Council Tax
   b. Credit Card Statement
   c. Credit Memo
   d. Pay Stubs

2. **Which document type is available for the IQ bot processing under Automation Anywhere Enterprise Edition?**
   a. Packing List
   b. Transport Document
   c. Electricity Bill
   d. All of the above

3. **The second stage of the IQ bot learning instance creation is _____.**
   a. Classification
   b. Production
   c. Upload
   d. Train

Answer

1. *c*
2. *d*
3. *a*

CHAPTER 12
Workflows

Introduction

In this chapter, a graphical approach to create automation will be discussed which is known as **Workflows**. A workflow provides a graphical view of the execution of the automation and also the process flow based on the specified conditions. A Workflow Designer is the interface provided to create workflows.

Structure

In this chapter, we will discuss the following topics:

- Workflow
- Creating workflows
- Workflow designer

Objectives

After completing this chapter, you should be able to:

- What are workflows
- Understand how to create the workflow
- Understand how to use the Workflow Designer

Workflows

A workflow is a mechanism provided by Automation Anywhere using which you can create your business process automation in a graphical environment. Alternatively, it can be said, a workflow provides you a high level, graphical view of your business process automation.

A Workflow Designer is an interface provided to create workflows. The four design objects provided in the workflow designer to create the workflows are as follows:

- **Start:** The starting point of the workflow; there can only be one Start design object in a workflow.

- **Run Task:** This the Run Task subcommand under the **Task** command that has already been discussed in *Chapter 7: Command Library*. You can plug multiple tasks together one after the other to create the workflow. Each Run Task design object has a successful and unsuccessful branch object.

- **If (Condition):** If is the conditional construct design object provided in the Workflow Designer to set the execution of the workflow based on whether the condition is true or false. It is the If-Else command discussed in *Chapter 7: Command Library*.

- **End:** It is the endpoint of the workflow. Each of the design object branches should be closed with End design objects.

Open the client application and select **Workflows** option on the left-bottom corner as follows:

Figure 12.1: Client Application | Workflows option

Click on the **New Workflow** option on the right-hand side top corner to open **Workflow Designer** window as follows:

Figure 12.2: Client Application | Workflows | New Workflow option

The Workflow Designer window has options like **Start, Run Task, If, End, New, Save, Validate, Run,** and **Variable Manager** as shown in the following figure:

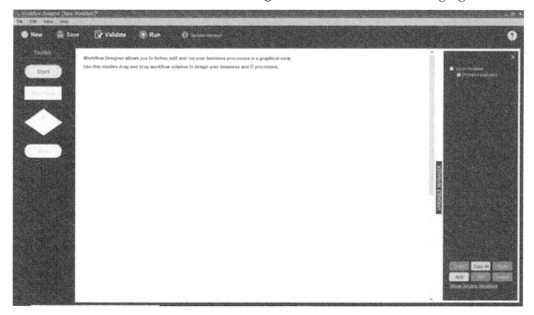

Figure 12.3: Workflow Designer window

In the Workflow Designer window, drag and drop the **Start** design object as follows:

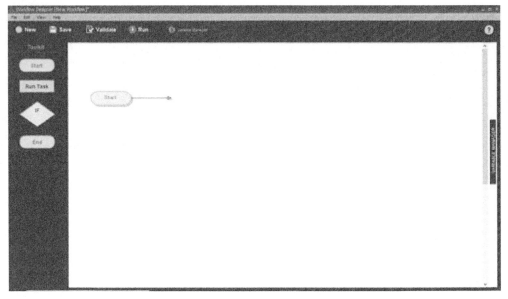

Figure 12.4: Workflow Designer | Start design object

Use the If design object to open the **If-Else** window, which has the same options as discussed in *Chapter 7: Command Library*. Select the **File Exists** option and click on the **Browse** button to select the Attendence.txt file that was generated during the creation of the **Keystrokes** command task and click on the **Save** button as follows:

Figure 12.5: Workflow Designer | If the design object

The True and False branches will be created attached to the If design object after you click on the **Save** button as follows:

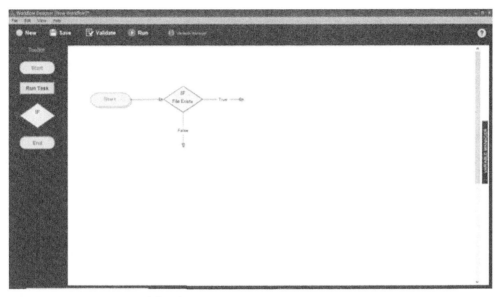

Figure 12.6: *Workflow Designer | If design object with true and false branches*

Now, drag and drop the **Run Task** design object next to the **True** branch in the **Workflow Designer** window to open the **Run Task** window, which has the same option as discussed during the **Run Task** command in *Chapter 7: Command Library* and now, select the task created for the **Keystrokes** command and click on the **Save** button as follows:

Figure 12.7: *Workflow Designer | Run Task design object*

The `Successful and Unsuccessful` branches will be created which is attached to the **Run Task** design object after you click on the **Save** button as follows:

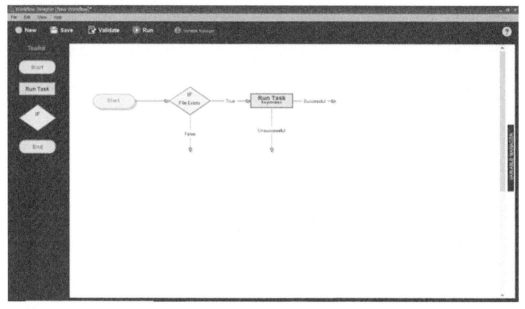

Figure 12.8: *Workflow Designer | Run Task design object with successful and unsuccessful branches*

Now, close all the open branches with the **End design** object to complete the workflow as follows:

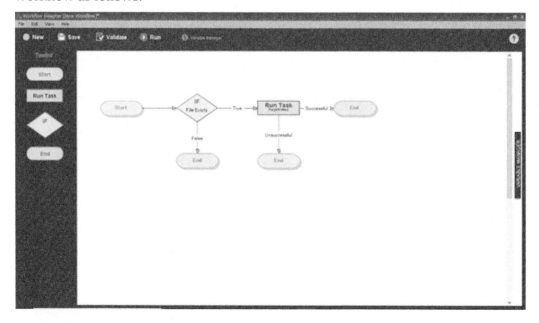

Figure 12.9: *Complete workflow design*

Click on the **Validate** button on the top to check whether the workflow has been created correctly and all the branches have been closed and click on the **Save** button to save the workflow, then click on the **Run** button to execute the workflow as follows:

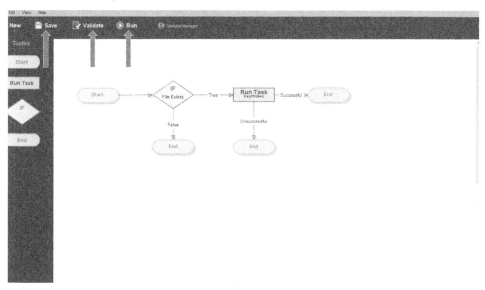

Figure 12.10: *Validate, Save and Run button*

Only the value type variable can be created in the Workflow Designer as follows:

Figure 12.11: *Only value type variable*

The same method can be used to create a workflow for complex business process automation in a graphical environment.

Conclusion

In this chapter, we discussed the workflows that are business process automation created in the graphical environment and the interface used to create workflows is known as the Workflow Designer. The Workflow Designer has four design objects, namely, Start design object for indicating the start point of workflow, Run Task design object for plugging the task logic of your automation, If design object for executing the task logic based on the conditions, and End design object for closing the branches and indicating the exit of the workflow.

Only the value type variables can be created in the Workflow Designer, and it is a best practice to validate your workflow before the execution using the **Validate** button provided on the top in the Workflow Designer window.

In the next chapter, we will discuss the system and audit logs that help in monitoring and troubleshooting the bots.

Multiple choice questions

1. **Which are the design objects provided in the Workflow Designer to denote the entry and exit of the workflow?**
   a. Start, Stop
   b. Start, Exit
   c. Start, End
   d. None of the above

2. **Which are the branches created when the If design object is created?**
   a. Correct, Incorrect
   b. True, False
   c. Yes, No
   d. None of the above

3. **The only type of variable that can be created in the Workflow Designer is _____.**
   a. string
   b. password
   c. array
   d. value

Answer

1. *c*
2. *b*
3. *d*

CHAPTER 13

System and Audit Logs

Introduction

In this chapter, we will discuss the system and audit logs that help in monitoring and troubleshooting. These logs are used to check and monitor the successful and failed execution of the bots. The logs are also used for inspection and refinement of the bot logic and to also help the support team to perform the bot execution perfectly by removing any issues in the bot when transferred to the production environment.

Structure

In this chapter, we will discuss the following topics:

- Logs and their importance
- System logs
- Audit logs

Objective

After completing this chapter, you should be able to:

- Understand about the logs and their importance in monitoring, troubleshooting, and maintaining the compliance
- Understand about the system logs

- Understand about the audit logs

Logs

The log files capture some very important data that is quite valuable for monitoring and troubleshooting. The log files capture the data about the activities being performed on the Web Control Room and the client application. The log files generated are of two following types:

- **System logs:** The log files that are generated on the client and that capture the data about the activities performed through the client application are known as the **system logs**.

- **Audit logs:** The log files that are generated on the Web Control Room and that capture the data about the activities performed through the Web Control Room are known as that **audit logs** and are available under a separate tab named Audit Log.

System logs

In the client application, under the **Tools** menu item, click on the **System Logs** submenu item to open the System Logs window as follows:

Figure 13.1: Client application | Tools | System Logs

Under the **System Logs** window, choose the type of logs you want to generate using the **Select Log Type** option and then, select the date range for which the logs have to be generated by using the **Start Date** and **End Date** options and then click on the **Generate Logs** button to display the logs in the **System Logs** window as follows:

Figure 13.2: *System Logs window*

The types of logs that can be generated under the system logs are as follows:

- All
- Task Creation
- Task Run
- Task Modification
- Task Deleted
- Workflow Creation
- Workflow Run
- Workflow Modification
- Workflow Deleted
- Report Creation
- Report Run
- Report Modification
- Report Deleted

- Task to Exe
- Schedule
- Trigger
- Task Properties
- App Configuration
- File
- Folder
- Script
- Other

If you want to export the logs to a CSV file, provide the name of the CSV file along with the full path for the file to be created and then click on the **Export** button at the bottom. The default path is `C:\Users\username\Documents\Automation Anywhere Files\Filename.csv`, the same path that is accessed through the `ApplicationPath` system variable.

If you want to delete an entry, you can check the box next to the entry and then click on the **Delete** button.

Audit logs

Audit logs provide the information about the actions being performed through the Web Control Room. It provides the administrator with the important information about the entities (Bot Creator, Bot Runner, and Web Control Room users) actions like user creation, modification, deletion, enabling, disabling, logins, logout, and so on and also system actions like backup and more along with the successful and unsuccessful action to ensure security and compliance at the enterprise level as follows:

Figure 13.3: Audit Log page

We can perform the actions listed as follows on the audit log page:

- **Filter Data**: The data can be filtered based on the time with the default option being the Last 24 hours and the other options provided being **Custom**, **Last 7 days**, **Last 30 days**, **Last 60 days**, and **Last 90** days. The additional data filters provided are **Status**, **Action type**, **Item name**, **Action taken by**, **Source device**, **Source**, and **Request ID**.

- **Search**: You can search for the data based on the filters provided and can also combine the phrases within the double quotes to search the exact phrase.

- **Export Data**: The data of the selected entry or entries can be exported to the CSV file by clicking on the **Export** icon in the right-hand side corner just succeeding the search box.

- **View Audit Details**: The details of an audit entry can be checked by clicking on the three-dot button and the Audit Details icon at the end of the entry on the right-hand side.

The audit log has a role-based access so only the administrator or user with the audit log privileges can access the audit log page and view the details.

Conclusion

In this chapter, we discussed the logs and the importance of the logs for monitoring, troubleshooting, maintaining security, and ensuring compliance. The logs generated at the client level are known as the *system logs* and are available in client application under the Tools menu item and System Logs submenu item. The logs generated for the entity actions on the Web Control Room are known as the *audit logs* and are available under the audit log tab and can be accessed only by the administrator or a user with the audit log privileges.

After completing the chapter, we can now check the system logs generated at the client level that are available in the client application and audit logs that are available on the Web Control Room.

In the next chapter, we will discuss uploading the bot from the client application to Web Control Room and then scheduling the bot from the Web Control Room, so that the bot can be executed on the Bot Runner.

Multiple choice questions

1. **Which type of logs can be generated under the System Logs window?**

   a. Script

   b. Task Deleted

   c. Workflow Creation

   d. All of the above

2. **Which filters are available under the audit logs?**
   - *a.* Task
   - *b.* Column
   - *c.* Time
   - *d.* None of the above

3. **Which options are provided in a time-based filter under the audit logs?**
   - *a.* Last 7 days
   - *b.* Last 90 days
   - *c.* Custom
   - *d.* All of the above

Answer

1. *d*
2. *c*
3. *d*

CHAPTER 14

Bot Transfer and Scheduling

Introduction

In this chapter, you will learn to upload the bots to the Web Control Room and then download the bots to the Bot Runner. You will also learn about scheduling the bots for execution on the Bot Runner.

Structure

In this chapter, we will discuss the following topics:

- Uploading the bots
- Downloading the bots
- Scheduling the bots

Objectives

After completing this chapter, you should be able to:

- Understand how to upload and download the bots
- Understand how to schedule the bots for execution on the Bot Runner

Bot Transfer

Once the bots are created, they have to be uploaded from the Bot Creator to Web Control Room and then downloaded on the Bot Runner machines, and then these bots are scheduled on the Web Control Room to be executed on the Bot Runner immediately or at a later stage.

Login into the client application with the Bot Creator credentials. There are three ways to upload the bots to the Web Control Room. The first way to upload the bots is to select the bot you want to upload, right-click on it, and then click on the **Upload** option as follows:

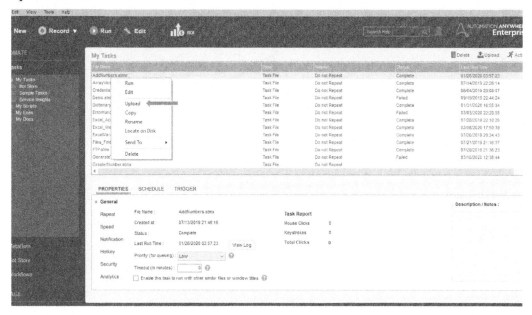

Figure 14.1: *Right-click the bot | Upload option*

The second way to upload the bot is to select the bot and then click on the **Upload** button at the top-right corner as follows:

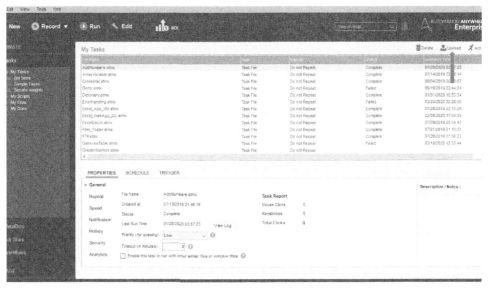

Figure 14.2: *Select the bot | Upload option at the top right corner*

You can upload the bots only one at a time using the aforementioned ways. Using the third way, you can upload one or multiple bots at the same time. Under the **Manage** option, select the **Repository** option on the left side to open the **Repository** window. Select the bots you want to upload from the bots available under the **Client Repository** and click on the **Upload** button as follows:

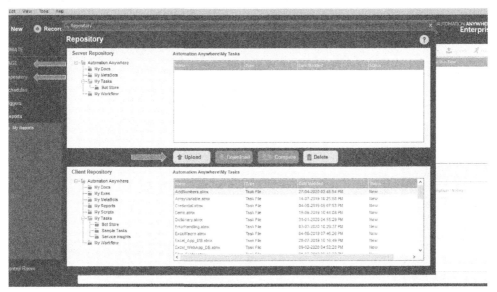

Figure 14.3: *Manage | Repository | Select Bot | Upload*

Once the bot is uploaded, you will be able to see the bot in the **Server Repository** as follows:

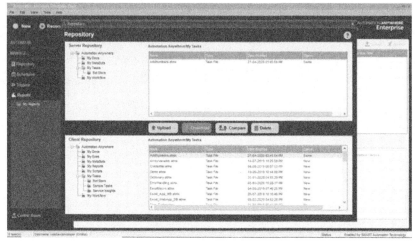

Figure 14.4: *Manage | Repository | Upload bot in Server Repository*

These are the three ways to upload the bots from the Bot Creator to Web Control Room. The third way is also used to download the bots on the **Bot Runner** from **Web Control Room** by selecting the bot on **Server Repository** and clicking on the **Download** button.

Scheduling

Under the **Tools** menu, select the **Re-Login** submenu option to login to the client application using the login credentials of the **Bot Runner** user created in *Chapter 4: Client Application* as follows:

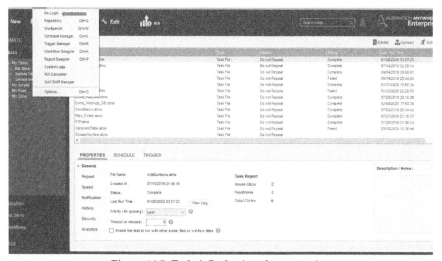

Figure 14.5: *Tools | Re-Login submenu option*

Login to the Web Control Room using the admin user credentials, and under the **Activity** tab, select the **Scheduled** option to schedule the execution of the uploaded bot. Click on either the schedule a bot option on the center of the page or click on the arrow next to the **Run bot** option at the top-right corner and select the **Schedule Bot** option from the dropdown list as follows:

Figure 14.6: Web Control Room | Activity | Scheduled | Schedule Bot option

Select the bot from the list under the **Bots** tab and **My bots** option and then, click on the right arrow button and then, click on the **Next** button as follows:

Figure 14.7: Web Control Room | Bots | My bots | Bot selection

There are two scheduling option provided as follows:

- **Run once:** The bot will be scheduled to be executed only once on the date and time provided under the **Start Date** and **Start Time,** respectively, as follows:

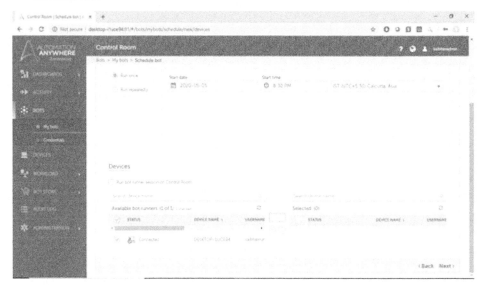

Figure 14.8: Web Control Room | Bots | My bots | Schedule Bot | Run once schedule option

- **Run Repeatedly:** The bot will be scheduled to be executed repeatedly between the dates provided in the **Start Date** and **End Date** option and the **Repeat** options being **Daily**, **Weekly**, and **Monthly** available.

The following is the sample of the **Repeat** option: **Daily**

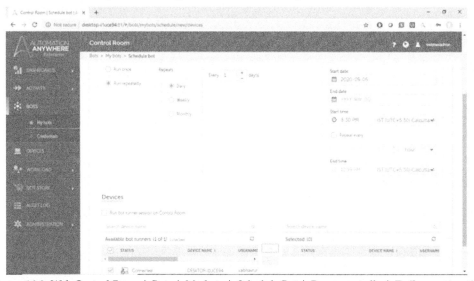

Figure 14.9: Web Control Room | Bots | My bots | Schedule Bot | Run repeatedly | Daily repeat option

The following is the sample of the **Repeat** option: `Weekly`

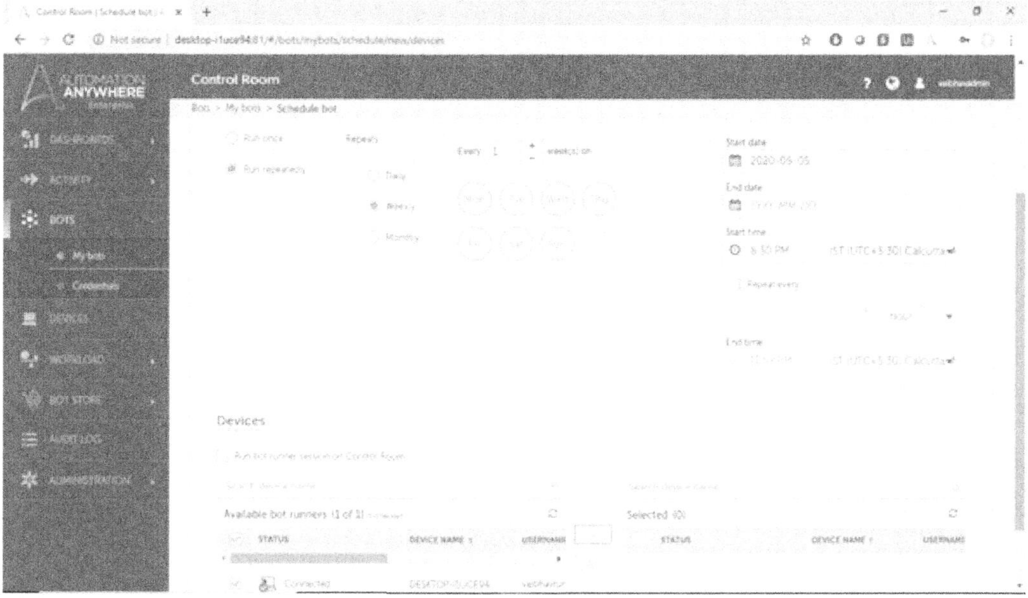

Figure 14.10: *Web Control Room | Bots | My bots | Schedule Bot*
| Run repeatedly | Weekly repeat option

The following is the sample of the **Repeat** option: `Monthly`

Figure 14.11: *Web Control Room | Bots | My bots | Schedule Bot |*
Run repeatedly | Monthly repeat option

Once you have selected the scheduling option then under the **Available Bot Runners** list, select the **Bot Runner** machine on which the bot is to be executed and click on the right arrow and then, click on the **Next** button as follows:

Figure 14.12: Bot runner selection

Click on the **Schedule bot** on the top-right corner to schedule the bot as follows:

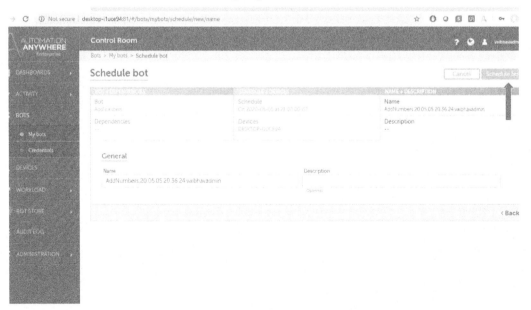

Figure 14.13: Bot scheduled

The bot will be available under the **Activity** tab and **Scheduled** option until the bot is executed. During the execution of the bot, it will be available in the **In progress** option and **Historical** option under the **Activity** tab after the execution of the bot.

Conclusion

In this chapter, we discussed about uploading a single bot and multiple bots at a time from the Bot Creator to Web Control Room and download the bot on the Bot Runner from the Web Control Room. We also discussed about scheduling the bot from the Web Control Room to be executed on the Bot Runner with either Run once or Run repeatedly options.

After completing this chapter, we can transfer the bot from the Bot Creator to Web Control Room and then schedule the bot from the Web Control Room to be executed on the Bot Runner.

Now, having completed the book, let us look back at the journey. We started with learning about the business process automation, then learnt about robotic process automation and the tools available in the market, then Automation Anywhere Enterprise Architecture, involving the Bot Creator, Web Control Room, and Bot Runner. Next, we learnt about the client application. After that, we learnt about the system and user variables and the five types of user variables that are value, list, array, random, and dictionary. Next, the standard use case was implemented which were excel data processing, web data extractor, stock price infuser, database data extractor, and invoice processing. Next, we learnt about the commands in the command library. Next, we learnt about the Metabots for the DLL execution and capturing objects in standard and remote, virtual machine (VM), Citrix and SAP environment, recorders namely screen, web, and smart, credential variables to store secure information, the IQ bots for classifying the documents and extracting data using cognitive capabilities and workflows, providing a graphical interface for creating a process flow. Next, we learnt about the system and audit logs and then in the final chapter, we learnt about the bot transfer and bot scheduling.

Multiple choice questions

1. **What is the path to upload multiple bots at the same time on the Web Control Room?**
   a. Manage | Schedules
   b. Manage | Reports
   c. Manage | Repository
   d. None of the above

2. The scheduled bots during the execution of the bot are available under the _____ tab in the Web Control Room.

   a. Activity | Historical

   b. Activity | In progress

   c. Activity | Scheduled

   d. None of the above

3. The scheduled bots after the execution of the bot are available under the _____ tab in the Web Control Room.

   a. Activity | Historical

   b. Activity | In progress

   c. Activity | Scheduled

   d. None of the above

Answer

1. *b*

2. *a*

3. *a*

Index

Printed in Great Britain
by Amazon

75415443R00156